Storyteller

THREE /// OWLS
PUBLISHING

EDITORS
Emerald Martinez
Shay Shivecharan

COVER
Photographer: Jeannie Albers
Author: Jonathan Rayson-Locke

 storytellermag.com

 info@storytellermag.com

 fb.com/storytellermagazine

 @storytellermagazine

---

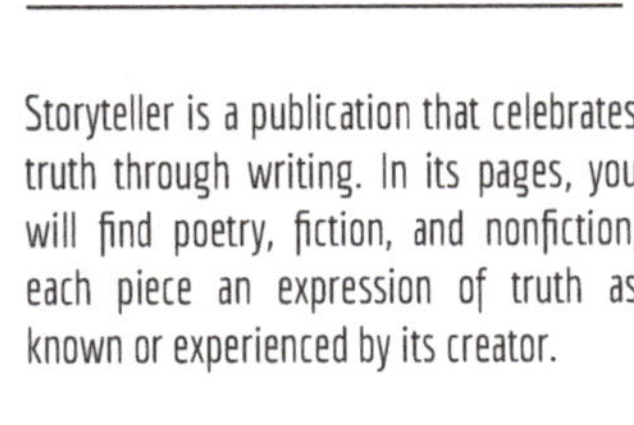

Storyteller is a publication that celebrates truth through writing. In its pages, you will find poetry, fiction, and nonfiction, each piece an expression of truth as known or experienced by its creator.

JEANNIE

ART DIRECTOR &
PHOTOGRAPHIST

ALBERS

JEANNIEALBERS.COM
JEANNIE@JALBERSSTUDIO.COM

POETRY

FICTION

NONFICTION

AUTHORS

Isabel Baylie Ericson @isabelericson

Isabel is a Swedish-American molecular biology student. Her left brain leads in the lab during the day, while her right composes lyrics, poetry, and paintings in the night. Growing up, she adored deciphering songs by Syd Barrett, Lou Reed, Leonard Cohen, Morrissey, and others, which eventually led to poetry writing. Her inspirations include Robert Frost, transcendentalist poets, and many musicians. Isabel has been writing poetry for 10 years and hopes to publish her own collection one day soon.

Gabrielle Roessler @habituallygabby

Gabrielle is a creative sprinter - she writes poems, short stories, and essays that prove she made great returns on her therapy investments. She has micro appearances with *Orange Blush Zine*, and forthcoming work in *Warning Lines*, *Hyacinthus Magazine*, and *Sledgehammer Lit*. She is inspired by myth, magical girls, a healthy fear of space, and overheard conversations that never happened.

Londyn Rayne @londynrayne

Londyn Rayne is a songwriter, lyricist, music producer, and a performing member in the band Sunset Roulett. She is also the founder of Orlando based ministry Label Me His. An advocate for mental/emotional health and healing, Londyn finds comfort in connecting with the power of words and expressing her pain and passions creatively whether it be through music, poetry or photography. She is soon releasing her first poetry collection and believes vulnerability is the beautiful beginning of transformation.

Aaron Morrison @theaaronmorrison

Aaron was born during the great __natural disaster__ in the __season__ of __year__. He spends his free time exploring __unusual location__ and raising domesticated __fictional creature(plural)__. One day, he would like to __verb__ his way to __place__ and try the various __noun(plural)__.

Blake Slaughter @blakeeslaughter

Blake Slaughter, born in Orlando and raised in Clermont, Florida, has had a passion for writing since he was eleven. Envisioning stories of horror and drama, he took up writing and hasn't stopped. He attributes a lot of his inspiration to music, varying from Frank Sinatra to Led Zeppelin. Other inspirations include authors Stephen King and William Peter Blatty, poets Edgar Allan Poe and Walt Whitman- most notably his poem "I Sing the Body Electric"- and the American film director Stanley Kubrick.

Emerald Martinez @emi_martinez1194

Emerald is a devourer of books and library enthusiast who has spent half her life in the Northeast and half in Florida. She obtained her Bachelor's in English from Boston University where she also studied Creative Writing. Prior to BU she studied at Valencia College where she acted as Phoenix Literature Magazine's Editor in Chief. Emerald hopes to pursue her Master's in Library Sciences and works as an Editor for Three Owls Publishing.

Cole Reeves @nicholasmichaelreeves

Nicholas "Cole" Reeves, 23, does not like the word writer, but does love to write. His heroes are Billy Collins, Gregory Alan Isakov, Ray Bradbury, Le Petit Prince, and of course, his mother. In 2018, he graduated from Stetson University with a degree in finance. He currently works at Lockheed Martin in Orlando, FL, on the Javelin missile, but poetry is his true love. He has a book club in Winter Garden, called The Paper Cuts. You can reach him at nmreeves2@gmail.com if you'd like to join the party.

Lisa Bui @nyugen.lisa.bui

Lisa Bui is a Hospitality and Tourism Management student and lives out her passion part-time as a barista when she's not cramming for project deadlines. She loves the spirit of the guest-oriented working environment but also enjoys some down-time with salsa classes, blog writing, and crime series marathons. Lisa dreams of opening her own coffee and pastry shop one day and use it as a platform to advocate for youth education and mental health awareness..

Joshua Mahn @joshmahnwrites

Joshua Mahn was the leading actor in not only "The Wicker Man", but also "National Treasure" and "Ghost Rider!" What's more, he lives inside your mirror and can not be removed.

He likes to make Fabergé eggs when he has some free time, or you can find him at your local pool next to the emergency floatation devices.

Jonathan Rayson-Locke

Jonathan Rayson-Locke is a barista and writer based in Winter Garden, FL. He attended Valencia College where he obtained his AA, and he is in the process of resuming his education at the University of Central Florida. When he is not writing stories, reading speculative fiction, or watching *Naruto*, he enjoys trying out new foods, being a plant daddy, and doom scrolling on "the bird app". You can find him on Twitter @j_nerdy_.

Seth Kaye @iamsethkaye

Seth Kaye is learning to be a poet. Though predisposed to the misconception that poetry is either world-alteringly legendary or utterly worthless (with no space in between), he has tasked himself with cultivating the elusive terrain in the middle. Devoted to the art of songwriting, Seth has only recently allowed himself to indulge in the writing of poems sans musical accompaniment. Fueled by a passion for language and the lyrical expression of human experience and emotion, he is on his way.

Gabriel McLeod @gabrielmcleod

Gabriel McLeod hails from a southern town intersected by railroads and rivers, canopied by magnolia and moonlight. He was born from a family of hard workers, dreamers and storytellers. He currently is working on a collection of short stories, a book of poetry, and the beginning stages of a novel. Gabriel made Orlando his home over 20 years ago and proudly lives with two extraordinary daughters and two enigmatic cats in a house with full bookshelves in every room.

Alex Gurtis @apbq_alex

Maryland born but Florida bred, Alex is a poet and journalist based in Orlando. His work has appeared in the *EcoTheo Review*, *Rejection Letters*, *Variety Pack*, *Montana Mouthful*, among others. A believer in leaving the world a little better than we found it, Alex is the founder of the Orlando Chess Club, a local 501(c) that strives to change lives through the facilitation of chess. Alex is a MFA candidate at the University of Central Florida.

Storyteller is always looking for new voices and fresh perspectives. Submissions can be made to: **storytellersubmissions@gmail.com**

MEOW

by Cole Reeves

If metaphors had calories, I'd be one full lad this morning.
I'm still in my boxers and the sun as I've explained to my cat
is a golden rose pinned to the pink coat of an angel.
Dawn, dear kitty, is the pink coat, but papa (as she knows me)
don't know no angels.

The thesaurus, I went on, is an old dinosaur,
just like its name sounds. It was the only of its kind
to survive the meteors, but evolved to live a quiet existence, feasting
mostly on the egos of grad students, textbook writers and people who don't
understand that less, in fact, is more.
Thesauri kill their prey by shoving words down their throats.

At most of these murder scenes, you can see predator
thesaurus sitting idly by on a table or a shelf, white hands
wide-open, as their victims slowly choke on words like
sesquipedalian loquaciousness,
which simply means, *the usage of a lot of long words.*
All those syllables get caught in the wind-pipe and
the curtain closes for good.

What I like about you, cat, is that you have
one word, *one* syllable, for everything.
And you're smarter than all of them, yes,
the whole damn bunch put together.

MY DOOR IS UNLOCKED

by Isabel Baylie Ericson

I don’t lock my door anymore
I don’t know who I thought I was

with shutters drawn taking in sunlight through a window

Gripping all I own
How my fingers ached
How terribly I wanted more

But today I live with my fingers spread
They would reach each corner of a room
If a room contained me

My door is unlocked and I float through the city
My palms are wide with nothing inside them
I bend back until I wrap around the Earth

My door is unlocked and my arms extend into forever

There is nothing in my hands
It is the Earth which holds me

DANCING AND DYING AT THE COCONUT CLUB

BY JONATHAN RAYSON-LOCKE

For some like Esther Durosier, this was the best night of the week

---

They looked forward to taking the hands of strange men, practicing their moves beneath the white lights to the pulse-pounding congas as they lost their sense of balance from a few sips of the fountain of youth.

But for Winston Patterson, there was no night he dreaded more.

"Lighten up," said Esther. "We're gonna have fun tonight, okay? Remember, *you* insisted we come here. To find the meaning of life."

Winston tried hard to tamp down the bitterness raging in his chest. He stared at her, hoping she didn't catch the evil eye he casted on her. She was a dark-skinned Haitian woman, fresh out of graduate school, and it was clear from her bouncy gait and red dress hanging tightly to her full frame that she meant to dance all her school troubles away. It was a shame that she couldn't dance *his* troubles away while she was at it.

"We can still go home," he said. "There's a new show I've been meaning to try –"

"Too late," said Esther. "The meaning of life is here. And we're finding it."

She traipsed away, her heels sending claps into the night. He sighed and followed her, walking up the steps of the building. The Coconut Club was the finest lounge in south Florida, but only wizards could tell that story. To the non-magical folk that milled around outside, dressed to kill as they stumbled to their own clubs, this one looked like an old, decrepit church pulled straight from the stucco and wood-laden annals of medieval Spain. But the bumping got louder as he ascended, reminding him that prayer was the last thing he'd be doing tonight.

Salsa music blasted him as he stepped inside. The booming tumbao bass line sent shivers down his spine. It didn't help that Esther started cheering as soon as she'd crossed the threshold. The place was already filled to near capacity, expert dancers leaving it all on the floor while old stragglers that pined for younger days made their way to the bar. Spicy-sweet perfume hung in the air like sheets and he raised his arm to shield his nose. With all the incense he'd burned in his spiritual practices, he should've been used to this by now. But he coughed anyway. This place reeked.

Esther plunged into the crowd before Winston could muster the courage to descend the steps. Winston sighed, submerging himself into the crowd. He bumped into a few people. His long-sleeve button up shirt with a too-stiff collar rubbed against his shoulders and neck. If only he had a different shirt to wear. He'd told his ex-wife that he didn't like the shirt, that it fit too snug, but she never listened to his complaints. That was just one reason why, as of today, Giselle was a memory of the past.

Winston reached the bar after a long swim through the sea of sweaty bodies. He sat down heavily at the stool and immediately placed his face in his right hand. The bartender, a bald Latine man with a floral rosary tattooed loudly on his forearm, turned to him and smiled.

"Long day?" he said, leaning against the counter.

Winston closed his eyes.

"You don't even know," he said. The bartender laughed and reached for the cabinet. He tossed glowing potions on the bar, mixing and matching them until he had a martini glass of a blue-green liqueur that vibrated subtly on the counter.

"Fountain of youth," said the bartender. "On the house."

"It doesn't work," Winston mumbled, but he took it anyway and stole a sip. The alcohol chilled his throat on the way down, a sure sign that this was a magical concoction and not regular mortal liquor. He let the icy wave wash down his spine, taking quick, cool breaths that puffed from his mouth. The bartender smiled, pleased with himself. But what Winston said still stood. The fountain of youth didn't work for him.

He watched as one at a time, elderly dancers arrived for their turn. The bartender performed his same trick near them, slinging out one glass after another until most of the patrons held some of that useless drink in their hands. They downed it, and Winston watched as their clothing, once pressed tight against their frail bodies, began to fit their form more perfectly. Wrinkles smoothed, gray hair blended to black, and hunched backs stood up straight.

That was the power of the fountain of youth. Elderly lovers drank the potion and became young again, just for the night. Winston put his head back into his palm as the newly young lovers edged their way to the dancefloor where the live band had started a new song with a faster tempo.

"It does work," said the bartender, who'd returned to clean up the area. "At least, it does for people who are old in their bodies. But you? You're old in your soul. And no potion can fix that."

Winston almost let his head fall on the counter. He tried to steady the beating of his heart, but it didn't help that across the club a group of dancers had gathered in a circle and were shouting in each other's faces.

"The hell is going on over there?" said Winston. The bartender sighed.

"Just the usual racket," he said. "Nothing that magical security can't handle. But that's not your problem, is it? Drink up, young blood."

"Come on, man," Winston mumbled. "Don't you have something else? I heard you have a drink. The meaning of life. I'll pay for that one."

The bartender chuckled. "That was just a gimmick," he said. "For folks like you. What, you lost a bet you can't pay? Girl left you? Feeling far from God? Sorry, but there's only one drink for that."

He poured a shot of overproof rum. A mortal drink.

"This isn't going to help me with my divorce," said Winston. The bartender shrugged.

"Yet you're here. And I'm sure you're going to tell me in detail how this broad hurt you."

Winston almost let the story spill from his mouth. How Giselle, or Jezebel as his traditional Jamaican mother would tell it, had taken him for a romantic spin from the altar to a two-story house just to leave him for a rich stockbroker who, like her, was lily-white. How he'd never felt any connection with a woman like her, and now that she'd finalized the divorce he wouldn't find anyone to fill the gap she'd blown into his heart. But just as he was ready to bare his soul, a drunken girl careened out of the crowd and knocked the drink right out of his hand.

Winston jumped out of his seat as his rum spilled over his shirt. The woman gasped, balanced herself on the bar, and slapped her hand on his shoulder.

"Oh my God," she slurred. "I'm so sorry!"

She stank of alcohol, and not the weak kind. She teetered to the side, almost falling into one of the stools.

"You're good," he said. He took one look at her and couldn't help but notice how pretty she was. Long curls framed her head and fell to her shoulders, and she wore a short blue dress that complimented the gold pigment swiped above her eyes.

"Can I help you?" he said.

"Mmmm," she said, eyes darting up and down. "You're cute. Wanna dance?"

Winston's body chilled. "Umm," he said, shuffling his feet. "I'm not very good –"

"Oh, this boy can move!" bellowed the bartender. "I had to clean him up from the dancefloor just last week!"

The woman giggled and took his hand, dragging Winston towards the band. He looked over his shoulder and cast the evil eye at the bartender, who stood there with his head thrown back in laughter. Her hand tightened around his as she stumbled onwards. He was caught up in this strange woman's rhythm, and there was no way he could escape now.

Once she found a satisfying spot on the floor, she faced him and pressed her chest against his. The itchy fabric of his clothes rubbed against his skin as she ran her hand up his back, and when he leaned in he could smell cheap, fruity perfume from her neck. He swallowed his pride, remembering the lessons he'd taken with Esther. But they slipped to nothingness as he timidly put his left hand on her hip.

She laughed, and he smelled her drunk breath again. This time, he picked out her most recent drink in the alcoholic chaos: Florida Red, the potion of choice for the wild and free. He could craft that with his eyes closed. Half a pinch of Dead Sea salt. A tablespoon of honey-coated frog marinade. Boiled and cooled three times in succession. A drop of blue haint oil here, a smidgen of the devil's paprika there. A precise science. Hard to make, quick to explode.

Somehow, that was easier than dancing.

"*She jerked and stumbled, making more of a mess of herself than Winston. He almost smiled. This woman was free and unabashed and beautiful in her own way.*

But he fell into the steps, awkwardly at first, though not as awkward as her. She jerked and stumbled, making more of a mess of herself than Winston. He almost smiled. This woman was free and unabashed and beautiful in her own way. Perhaps she would know...

"What's your name?" he said as he leaned into her.

"Yaritza," she said. He almost didn't hear her above the shouting that escalated around the corner.

"Wanna sit down?" he said. Yaritza laughed, her long neck pulsing with each breath, but she didn't resist as he pulled her to one of the couches. She fell next to him, her thigh pressed just above his, her face so close to his neck he could feel the heat of her breath.

"You ever heard of the meaning of life?" he whispered. Yaritza hiccupped.

"Whaddyu mean?" she said. Winston leaned closer to her.

"How do you live when your life has no meaning?" he said. "How do you go on when the only thing that meant something to you is gone? What's the point?"

Yaritza laughed. "Oh, you're a philosophy major, aren't you?" she said. "You remind me of this one professor I had a long, long time ago. Tall, skinny, old, bald, all that stuff. He asked us that same question soooo many times."

Winston perked up. "And his answer? What did he say?"

Yaritza's head collapsed on his chest.

"I don't know," she said. "I dropped out."

Warmth filled his head. He looked away from her and closed his eyes as hard as he could, hoping that would repel the anxiety pouring into his mind. Why did he think some drunken wizard girl would answer his problem when his educated best friend and a wise-cracking bartender couldn't? But he needed those answers. He needed to know how to live, how to escape the endless drudgery of Netflix shows. How to feel something other than quick pleasure in meaningless sex. But here he was, sad in the club and not a single step closer to getting what he wanted.

"Hey!" someone called from across the floor. A burly man stomped over, his half-finished bottle of beer gripped tightly in his beefy hand. Winston took a breath, trying to remember the calming exercises his therapist had taught him just two days prior, but those lessons fled him as the guy got closer. Yaritza jerked to attention, peeling her thigh away from Winston's.

"Babe –" she started.

"What you doing with my girl?" the man roared. "The fuck is wrong with you, stupid ass?"

"Hey man," said Winston, holding up his hands. "I don't want any trouble –"

"Get the fuck up," said the man. He reached down and yanked Winston to his feet with one hand. His body tightened, tongue immediately moving to start an incantation under his breath. His mind spun furiously, running through all the possible ways he could attack. A sudden fiery wall of protection would do him well here, but centering his mind for a quick banishing might work too –

Some more people came over, the same group that had just been arguing in the corner. The big man had his hand raised, fist ready to strike, but he lowered it as another guy barreled forward and pushed him down. A brawl broke out around him, and Yaritza screamed as she tried to scamper away from her alleged boyfriend, who'd fallen on the couch.

"Winston!" he heard Esther yell, but he barely registered it amidst the chaos. His mind twisted, tunnel vision overtaking his eyes. Strong intentions burned within him, and he focused his mind's eye on it, seeing nothing but fire. His tongue flicked, the incantation spilling out, but he was punched in the chest right as the last few syllables were coming out of his mouth. He fell backwards, losing the words, but he'd conjured a fire anyways.

Yaritza screamed. She jumped from the couch, stumbling away as she narrowly avoided getting licked by the flames that popped up in weak spurts. The brawlers snapped to attention and shouted incantations, their own protective spells forming shields around them. The fire was gone just as quickly as it started, as if it had never been there at all.

But now, magic was added to the scuffle. Some of the fighters started shifting to their older selves, and only then did Winston realize he was up against seasoned wizards. He ducked as a fist swung towards him, sailing harmlessly past his head. But when he looked up, he noticed that the hand – and the body attached – was *translucent*. An older man stared back at him, dressed in a suit more fitting for a 1920s jazz lounge than a modern salsa club.

"What the hell?" he said. "Y'all are summoning *ancestors* to fight?"

The dead man swung some more, catching Winston in his jaw. He cried out as he stumbled back, hands flying up to his face.

"I know I did *not* just get punched in the face by a ghost," he said. Now he'd had enough. He balled his fists, ducking and weaving from the ghost's blows while saying the incantation again. This time, the spell landed true. Another blaze rose up, forming a solid wall of heat. The ghost shimmered, then dissipated. More screaming came from the other side, most of it from Yaritza's mouth, but it was the reversible incantation from the burly man that set him on edge.

"Wait!" he cried out, too late. The incantation ended, and the flames, dancing before, now turned to face Winston. Smoke billowed from the top, cutting off his air supply. He barely had time to cry for help before a separate incantation for a binding spell finished, hitting him right in the chest. His arms and legs snapped together, sending him tumbling to the ground.

Dangerously close to his own inferno.

His mind raced, but all at once, his mystical education left him. He struggled to move, struggled to roll, struggled to breathe as heat licked at his face. Tears filled his eyes, staining his cheeks. Was this how he was going out? With a fire to put an end to what was his sorry life? He closed his eyes, struggling to accept his fate. He'd come here to find the answer to his deepest yearnings, to find the meaning of life.

But at the end of it all, he'd forgotten to live.

He almost succumbed to the despair, but a banishing incantation sounded from a distance. The flames flickered then swallowed themselves out of existence, leaving only a charred floor behind. Winston's appendages loosened, and he groaned as his throat opened. He rolled over, body shaking. Just like that, he had survived. Just like that, he had another day to live.

"What the *fuck* is wrong with y'all?" said the bartender, strolling over red-faced. "Fighting in my club? And with *magic*? You want them to call the human police and shut this shit down?"

Winston stumbled to his feet, but the bartender grabbed him and got right in his face.

"How the fuck do you go from trying to find the meaning of life to starting a magic fight?" he spat. "Over an old woman?"

"Huh?" said Winston. The bartender twisted him around. Across the club on an empty section of the dancefloor, an elderly woman sat on her ass and sobbed.

While wearing Yaritza's dress.

Winston blinked. "Look, man –"

"I hope you find what you're looking for," said the bartender. "But it's not gonna be in here. Now get the fuck out of my club and don't came back!"

Winston tried to argue, but a sharp tug on his shirt stopped him. Esther dragged him away from the bartender and past the crowd of dancers, some of them still holding each other in the midst of the silence. He blinked as realization hit him. Had he really gotten into a fight with some old men? He let Esther yank and twist his collar, embarrassed that clubgoers in the costume of a younger generation had watched him throw hands at elderly people. The band started up just as he reached the exit, the lead singer saying something in Spanish that made the dancers laugh nervously. Winston missed the rest of the speech, the man's words swallowed up by car horns and a ferocious wind.

"Are you happy now?" said Esther. "Was that worth getting banned from the Coconut Club? After all we practiced?"

Winston almost said no, but he stopped himself. He couldn't help it. He felt *good*. All those months of emptiness, the slow-paced days, the tear-soaked nights... He'd forgotten it all in the thrill of the fight and the fear of death. The rush would fade and his heart would ache again, but for right now, he was alive.

Perhaps that was the meaning of life. To simply... live.

Winston perked up as Esther stomped down the stone steps. He caught up with her, putting his arm around her shoulder.

"Hey, I'm sorry," he said. "It was just a misunderstanding that got out of control, okay? I'm good."

"You owe me," she said. "And not cheap shit, either. Ruth's Chris, Fogo de Chao, something like that."

"I can do that," he said. "And you know, there's still that show I've been trying to finish…"

"No comfort sex for you, jerk," she said, throwing his arm off her. "You should've tried it with the grandma in there. I'm not the one."

Winston laughed and let her walk ahead to call for a car back into town. He stared at the club from the bottom of the staircase, amazed that a church so run-down housed something so magical. He had half a mind to walk back in there, apologize to the bartender, maybe try to see if he could at least get some lenience for Esther. But he'd try that another time, on another night. For now, he simply had to fulfill his purpose. He simply had to live.

He'd dreaded this night for days.

But maybe, just maybe, salsa night at the Coconut Club wasn't so bad after all.

the paradox, prey and hunter *by seth kaye*

while it rained i sat
and watched the water make no sound
such gentleness i feel
is only found in animals
some plants
and probably most good mothers
it's their gentle washing over
and their quiet running under
so often overlooked
by men who have life too easy
(just because, and because we are loud)
yet know nothing of feeding a child
slowly
from the fruit of our own body
why am i only now remembering
and waking up from dreams to remind myself
i have had a mother my whole life
and she has never hidden,
not once
because she is both a lamb and a lion
the paradox,
the prey and hunter
The Keeper of Life's keeper of life

Waking Up In Quarantine

by Alex Gurtis

---

1. Today is _?

    A. Another week of quarantine

    B. The day I stopped checking the clock

2. What are the new days of the week?

    A. Monday now means Wednesday

    B. Wednesday now means Friday

    C. Friday now means Monday

    D. Names no longer have meaning; a new day is the sun poking sagging eyelids urging you to live

3. What do we find when we get out of bed?

    A. There are no days of rest to be found, replaced with sleepless nights

    B. Mental unease is tracked by darting eyes

    C. Sunny days giving way to the perpetual rains of April

THE HITCHHIKER

by Cole Reeves

A thumb on the shoulder
of this old country road
knifing through the middle of hell Georgia.

And me -- no Good Samaritan.
Well I punch the pedal
after I see the unibrow
and those two-octave hands
gripping the duffel bag
bone-white tight.

Now, if I cared more about my poetry, I
would have given the hitchhiker a ride
in exchange for whatever madness of his
he might let me plagiarize.

But I am all the madness I need, tonight.
I'm just coming back from the dead cornfields,
scaring the crows, watching the stars swim,
giving the local paper a little something to talk about.

That's not to mention what happened two nights ago
in the abandoned farmhouse west of town.
Or last week, even, behind the ruins of the old coal mill.
where I caught those kids chain-smoking
like Oddfellows in an REM song.

Enough madness, I say
with a grin to the radio static,
and my ‘67 Ford coughs a hole through the Ozone.

I arrive at the barb-wire gate,
it crumples like tin-foil in the dark fists of the wind.

I leave the duffel bag on the seat.
My boots hit the dirt. I see in the headlights
a day-old morning paper, lying like a bone
in the yard.

Night is black as coffee, so
I put on a pot,
open up the paper,
pin it to the wall.

Another body
in another cornfield.

Coffee’s cold now, but I don’t mind.
Just a little pissed off, a little
pissed off and tired

of those damn writers.

They keep leaving out
the most important details.

Rx For a Dream

by Gabrielle Roessler

Dreams are the small drunken children
that stumble across the backs of my eyes
when blurry vision gives way
to darkness delivered by 5 milligram postmen.

I'm the suburban mother sipping Chardonnay
behind slick shades with my sunchair turned away
from the yard I should be watching.

Tiny chickens chased by fleet foxes
creating crimson splashes on the snow
in the grass I can't sweep or wash with bubbly.
The sensation of slipping on the wet
with that nauseating flip
on the last missed step
at the bottom of the stairs –

the jolt catapults me into a new scene
dripping with more
lingering unease.

Familiar faces twisted up at the ends
drive fear deeper.
It pulls me, pushes me, shoves me six feet down
and pins me at the edges by sharp feral points.
I'm digging through damp earth,
rot and petrichor and fermented grapes
thick in my throat,
gasping to life and blinding light
after another long, moonless night.

AUTHOR FOCUS

WITH JONATHAN RAYSON-LOCKE

Jonathan Rayson-Locke is 100% committed to the craft. For him, writing is part of his daily life and mission, and no longer just a hobby. Spurred on by a deep love of storytelling and a great appreciation for the accomplished writers who have come before him, Jonathan is well on his way to being a successful author himself. Outside of writing, he enjoys the company of family and friends, often while talking about books or sharing a good meal together. He is a big fan of all the other aspiring writers around him, and lends his wisdom and support whenever he can. We are very honored to have him on the cover and the chance to ask him a few questions about his writing journey.

Who is your favorite author and how have they influenced you as a writer?

I have two favorite authors, but the one I will focus on here is Brandon Sanderson. Not only is he an incredibly prolific speculative fiction writer, but he teaches a speculative fiction creative writing class at BYU and he posts his lectures on YouTube for free! Watching those lectures and reading his stories as an example of what he teaches has been instrumental in my formation as a writer. Without that, I can't tell you where I'd be. And his stories are also really good!

What part of the writing process comes easiest to you? What part is the hardest?

My favorite part of the writing process is hammering out the initial draft. During this stage, the words just flow. I feel free to make mistakes, to change directions as the story demands, and to just have fun with whatever world I am building. But the hardest part for me has always been the revision process. This is the part where I now have to take my hastily written story and make sense of it. All the pieces have to be put together in a way that is coherent and engaging to the reader, and I find it to be the most daunting part of writing stories.

As a Black author, do you feel as though the industry has become more inclusive and diverse in recent years? If so, who are the giants upon whose shoulders this movement stands, past and present?

The emergence of diverse (and particularly Black) speculative fiction has been one of the most exciting developments in the past five years. We are experiencing a Renaissance of sci-fi and fantasy where many of the books on the cutting edge of the genre are written by people from marginalized backgrounds, and every week there are more deals that are being announced and more books that are being published. I think the best example of this is my other favorite author, N.K. Jemisin. She is one of the most critically acclaimed Black woman speculative fiction writers, and she has finished multiple series that have cemented her as one of the staples of the genre. But for her and for other Black sci-fi and fantasy writers, these great gains would not be possible without the work of the literary genius Octavia Butler. She is one of the greatest writers to ever live, and I encourage anyone reading this to go and check out her work for yourselves.

How did the events of 2020, from COVID-19 to quarantine to the worldwide racial/social justice movement affect or inspire you as a writer?

When it comes to COVID-19, though my mental health took a hit like everyone else, I suddenly had a lot of time on my hands during the early days of the quarantine. I put it to good use by focusing on putting words to the page as fast as possible, and when I look back on all that I accomplished during that time, I have started to see the pandemic as something of a silver lining. And as for the various movements that have swept the world, my writing has always been informed by a commitment and passion for social justice, and the protests of 2020 served to galvanize me even more. I often think about the impact that the various forms of inequality have on the world, and as

I study solutions to how this could be addressed, this seeps into my writing. I find that to be one of the most beautiful aspects of speculative fiction; you can write a story about elves that heal or dragons that prophesize or space ships that fly to unknown worlds, but all such stories are grounded in the real world, and those stories have the ability to shape the real world for good.

You seem to be an avid student of the writing discipline as someone who actively seeks out and embraces the lessons and advice of accomplished writers, especially as it pertains to the more technical aspects of storytelling and world-building. Many writers tend to shy away from this kind of thing, convinced it may stifle their own creativity. Why is your view different?

My view of learning the technical parts of telling stories is that they don't stifle creativity. Instead, they enhance it. I believe that there is "secret sauce" that informs every brilliant piece of fiction, and peeling back the layers and learning the fundamentals of storytelling are key in replicating that brilliance. Writing is also a skill, and that skill can be perfected through mentorship from people further along in the craft. To me, there is no downside to breaking down the art of writing to its basic parts. I have found my ideas becoming more concrete as a result.

Can you tell us a little bit about the writing project you are most excited about working on this year?

As much as I love short stories, I am a novelist at heart. My current project is a mashup of epic fantasy and the dark academia trope, where a young man skilled in monster summoning attends a magic university where a fellow monster summoner is unleashing them on other students. For me, the most exciting part of this project is that it came to me out of nowhere, refused to let me go, and a draft was written three months later. Hopefully I'll have a coherent, edited draft finished by the end of the year. And I intend to have a lot of fun doing it!

Check out Jonathan's story, titled "Dancing and Dying in the Coconut Club", on page 8.

ELMHURST ASYLUM

BY AARON MORRISON

Two cars pulled up

and parked outside the fence that surrounded Elmhurst Asylum. While unlikely, there was a chance the cars could be spotted if parked right in front of the gate. They were some distance away from the building. It would be a walk up to the asylum itself, but the gates were locked and there was no other way to get to the building.

Aubrey, Donovan, Malik, and Anya stepped out of the front car. Brennon, Kelly, Mike, and Liv emerged from the second.

"So what's the deal with this place, Malik?" Brennon asked, coming around the back of the car and grabbing Kelly, his girlfriend, around the waist. "Is it haunted? Cause nothing gets Kelly's juices flowing like that spooky shit." Brennon gyrated his hips, rubbing up against Kelly, who laughed drunkenly.

Brennon, Kelly, and Mike all had open cans of beer in their hands. Their stumbling and slightly slurred speech made it clear they were drunk.

"You all were drinking on the drive over here?" Malik observed. Though not surprised, he was still in disbelief.

"What?" Brennon responded defensively as he shrugged, downing the rest of his beer. "Liv was driving."

Liv, Mike's girlfriend, half smiled. She shifted her stance constantly and kept her arms crossed. She avoided eye contact with the group, focusing her gaze away from the asylum.

"Get me another beer, Mike," Brennon demanded, too busy fondling Kelly to get one himself.

"Coming right up." Mike retrieved more cans from the car. "Anyone else want one?" He offered a can to the others. "Donovan?"

Donovan hesitated.

"Sure. Fine. I'll have one." Donovan threw his hands up in surrender and took the can from Mike.

"That's the spirit!"

Donovan popped open the beer, the distinctive *psssch* sound echoed out, and he tapped his can against Mike's. Donovan took a sip and meandered back to Aubrey, Malik, and Anya.

"To answer your question, Brennon," Malik continued on the original topic, "there's rumors about Elmhurst being haunted, of course. So much tragedy, neglect and horror. So I guess you could say it's definitely haunted. If not by ghosts, then by all the negative memories here."

Aubrey, Donovan, and Anya all exchanged smiles. They were all amused with Malik's passion. They'd heard all this before but never got tired of it. Malik's excitement and love for the history of these kinds of places was infectious. Anya was supportive of her boyfriend's pursuit in becoming a documentary filmmaker, and Aubrey and Donovan were encouraging of their friend.

"So what you're saying is this place was full of lunatics." Brennon took another drink.

"I wouldn't put it like that," Malik was a little taken aback, "but yeah. I guess."

"There aren't any patients still wandering around here, right?" Liv hugged her arms to her sides, rubbing her upper arms nervously. Her eyes darted around as if expecting someone to jump out of the darkness at any moment.

Malik shook his head. "Doubtful. Elmhurst was shut down and cleared out some sixty years ago, so it's pretty unlikely."

"Let's go check this freakhouse out then." Brennon chugged his beer and grabbed another one from Mike.

The group made their way towards a gap in the iron fence where they could squeeze through. Aubrey looked back and saw that Donovan had knelt down to tie his shoe. She thought it odd since it looked like Donovan's shoe was already tied. She watched him take his beer and pour most of it out on the ground and quickly looked away. She didn't want Donovan to know she'd caught him. She was kind of impressed, however, at his maneuver in keeping Brennon, Mike, and Kelly happy while avoiding getting drunk himself.

"Hey. Sorry," Donovan whispered to Aubrey after he had jogged back up to her and the group. "Had to tie my shoe."

They all shimmied through the gap in the fence and continued on towards the looming building.

Elmhurst Asylum was imposing, even rundown as it was. Shattered windows, though still barred, looked out from all three stories at the group like so many eyes. The large double doors waited to swallow them whole.

The light from the moon was surprisingly bright and gave decent illumination of the surrounding area.

"So this place *was* full of psychos then?" Brennon continued his inquiry.

"Stop referring to them all like that," Aubrey scolded, unable to hide her annoyance with Brennon anymore.

" Elmhurst Asylum was imposing, even rundown as it was. Shattered windows, though still barred, looked out from all three stories at the group like so many eyes.

"What?" Brennon was defensive. "You're telling me there *weren't* a bunch of sicko molesters and shit in there?"

"But that's the point. Everyone got lumped together into one category," She started. "Yeah, of course you had that kind of mentally damaged person sent here. But then you'd have anyone that had even relatively minor mental health issues, or people that were just different, dumped here and forgotten for things we probably wouldn't even think twice about today. How would you feel if you got left here with all the 'sickos,' as you called them, just because you were sad all the time, or something like that. And then you were abused or neglected here, either intentionally or due to lack of understanding or funding. Would that be fun, *bro*?" Aubrey emphasized the last phrase as mockingly as she could.

"Yeah. But I have my happy juice right here." Brennon shook his beer can.

"Jesus." Aubrey shook her head, frustrated that she had even tried to explain it.

Liv had grown increasingly scared and clung to Mike, who offered drunken, half-hearted reassurances of "It's all good, babe" and "Stop worrying".

Brennon returned to making comments of various degrees of explicitness towards Kelly. Malik discussed with Anya his vision for his documentary about Elmhurst. Aubrey and Donovan walked in silence. They stopped in front of the doors, which appeared to be the only elements of the asylum not in a complete state of decay. Malik pulled a small flashlight from his pocket.

"So, it's going to be pretty dark in there," he said. "Use flashlights if you brought 'em or use your phone."

"I don't have any service." Kelly looked at her phone.

"Me either," confirmed Mike.

"I mean, look around you." Malik gestured to the wide open sky and the surrounding woods. "We're basically in the middle of nowhere. No reason for cell towers out here."

"What if something happens?" Liv chewed at the corner of her lower lip.

"Nothing's going to happen." Brennon rolled his eyes. "Let's go."

Malik and Brennon pushed open the doors. They all stepped inside. The large lobby was cluttered and filthy. Upended rotten chairs, dirt, dust, and various debris littered the tile floor. Detritus from the rotting ceiling and walls had made little mountains of material scattered around the room. The stairway to the second floor was several yards ahead of them. Aubrey was certain the decay had started long before this place had been abandoned.

The group circled out. They moved past a large desk, maneuvering around the tipped over chairs, and peered into the reception office through the grimy glass. A few pictures and document frames still miraculously hung on the walls, quite possibly sealed to the wall with grime.

"Hey, Donno! I didn't know you worked here." Brennon was standing in front of a picture frame that hung on a wall. His voice boomed through the room.

"Real fucking funny, Brennon," Donovan responded.

"No, seriously." Brennon waved Donovan over. He tipped his beer can towards the picture.

A few of the group walked over to see what Brennon was on about. Behind the smudged glass, only somewhat visible through the streak Brennon had left after wiping away the dust and grime with the side of his hand, was an old photograph of a group of employees of Elmhurst Asylum. Doctors, nurses, orderlies, and other workers all standing in front of the asylum. One of the orderlies had a passing resemblance to Donovan.

"See?" Brennon was insistent. He wiped the dirt from the side of his hand on his jeans.

"I mean, maybe." Donovan squinted and looked closer. "If you squint and or close your eyes."

"Aubrey? Malik? You can't tell me that doesn't look like him."

"I guess a little bit," Malik conceded.

Aubrey could see a minor similarity between the man in the photo and Donovan, but it was so slight she didn't make anything of it.

"It's hard to tell," Aubrey shrugged. "Especially since now we're looking at it with that in mind. Besides, you're drunk. Not like I trust your analysis of old photographs."

Brennon pointed at Aubrey with his beer and then took another gulp.

"Very true," He laughed, and walked off to rejoin Kelly.

Aubrey and Donovan looked at the photograph again, then to each other. They both shrugged and went to catch up with the group.

"So, uh, how's the art going?" Donovan asked. "Any new projects?" He walked next to Aubrey, hands in his pockets, shoulders turned slightly in.

"It's good." Aubrey paused. "I mean. Sort of. Had a creative block for a while, honestly. It's frustrating."

Donovan nodded.

"I've gotten a few commissions, mostly corporate art and logos, which keeps the power on, but it's just I want to focus on my own thing, I guess? And it's like I haven't used my own voice in so long, I've forgotten how to speak."

"I can understand that. I mean, kind of. I'm definitely not an artist. I can draw a mean stick figure, but anything beyond that looks like a three year old with two broken arms drew it."

Aubrey laughed. Donovan smiled bashfully.

"For what it's worth," Donovan continued, "you're a talented artist. You'll find your voice again. Motivation, or whatever, comes out of nowhere sometimes, so, uh, don't give up. You know?"

"Thank you, Donovan." Aubrey smiled. Donovan nodded and smiled back.

They soon found themselves on the second floor of the asylum. The group looked into various rooms, exploring a bit, trying to be careful as the floor had given way in some places. The majority of the floor was patient housing. The rooms had thin, rotted mattresses on brittle metal frames. A few still had small, now destroyed dressers.

"I gotta piss," Mike said, breaking the silence, and started back to the stairs.

"Where you going?" Brennon asked.

"I thought I made that pretty fucking clear, bro."

"Go piss in the corner or something. Nobody's living here."

"Dude, I ain't that nasty. I'm just gonna go piss in the woods and I'll be right back."

Brennon scrunched his face and shook his head.

"Be careful, babe," Liv called, sounding nervous.

"*Be careful, babe.*" Brennon mocked, pitching his voice up.

"Asshole." Kelly smacked Brennon's arm and laughed.

"What? Haha. I'm just fucking around." Mike left to do his business and the group continued looking around the second floor.

After a few minutes passed, they came across a room with a crudely spray painted pentagram with the obligatory 666 above it. They had both been drawn hastily and without skill. The cheap, red spray paint dripped in places, like comically fake blood. A few half-melted candles were stuck to the floor in front of the satanic display.

"Looks like we found the edgelord room," Brennon observed.

As crass as Brennon was, the group didn't really disagree with him. There wasn't anything that indicated this was anything more than the stereotypical graffiti one tends to find in places like this.

"I still don't like it." Liv said, hugging herself tightly.

"Why do you think people always do stuff like that in places like these?" Aubrey wondered.

"Good question," Malik responded. "I mean, like Brennon said, it just seems like the edgy, cool thing to do. Go to an abandoned building. Smoke a little meth. Do a little Satan worship. Big time rebel shit." Malik chuckled. "Though I think, in some cases, people are attracted to places like these *because* of the negative vibes. Places with misery seem like good places to call on evil. Breeding ground for ghosts and such. Real or imagined."

Brennon tossed his crushed beer can on the ground. It clattered and skidded to join the rest of the trash on the floor. The sound of him spitting followed. With that, the group left the room and headed back down the hall towards the front of the building. They poked their heads into a few rooms and saw more of the same patient residences they had already seen.

"Ummm, guys? Come here," Anya called, standing in front of the broken window that overlooked the front yard of the asylum. She was looking down at something, a look of concern on her face.

"What is it?" Malik asked.

"Someone's standing out there."

"What?" Several of them said in unison.

The group gathered close to Anya and looked out onto the grounds.

There, illuminated in the moonlight, stood a figure concealed by a slightly baggy, greyish-blue jumpsuit, and a full head mask. Seeing someone standing still and staring at them was unnerving enough, but the mask made it all the more terrifying.

The mask looked like it was made of tanned, dried flesh with small silvery studs along the mouth and eye sockets. The featureless face was disturbing and dehumanizing.

Aubrey felt more sick than scared looking at it.

"Who is that?" Kelly asked.

"It's probably Mike fucking around. Why'd he say he was going all the way to the woods to piss?" Brennon spoke with drunken certainty. "Probably went to play dress up. And if it's some random creep, I'll beat the shit out of him." Brennon leaned out the window. "Hey douchebag! Real fucking scary, bro! It's a good way to get your ass kicked!"

The figure gave no signs of response.

"What do we do?" Liv began to panic.

"What do you mean?" Brennon was incredulous. "Like I said, it's probably your boyfriend being a dick."

"But what if it's not?" Liv's voice wavered. Her breathing had increased. "What if, what if it's..."

"What? One of Malik's loonies? Then he's going to get what's coming to him." Brennon pushed past the group. "Either way, I'm not staying here all fucking night."

Kelly followed after him. Malik and Anya glanced at each other, and then to Aubrey, Donovan, and Liv. Aubrey had placed her arm around Liv's shoulders in an attempt to reassure and calm her.

"I mean, I guess let's go down." Malik stammered. Donovan shrugged and nodded. The five of them made their way down the stairs and to the front door where Brennon stood just outside the doorway.

"Mike!" Brennon was shouting at the figure. "You had your fun, bro!" The figure stared dead ahead and gave no response. "Don't think I won't kick your ass, man. And if you aren't Mike, it's gonna be even worse."

Nothing.

"Man. Fuck this." Brennon started to march forward. His fists balled up in rage. "One last chance, motherfucker."

A few paces from the figure, Brennon raised his right fist. He closed the distance, ready to pummel the figure. The figure's right hand moved. Something glinted in its hand before being thrust into Brennon's stomach.

The group watched as Brennon's body tightened and bent forward.

There was what felt like an eternal pause before the figure gripped Brennon's shoulder with his other hand and drove a silver instrument into Brennon's stomach again and again.

The sickening *shunk, shunk, shunk,* and Brennon's gurgling and gasping was soon drowned out by Kelly and Liv's screams.

"Shit! Shit! Shit! What the fuck? Back inside! Back inside!" Malik yelled at everyone, pushing them backwards.

Malik and Donovan slammed the doors shut and dragged a nearby desk flush against them. Aubrey had both arms around Liv, who was now sobbing and screaming hysterically. Anya tried to tend to Kelly, who was shaking with shock.

"What do we do, man?" Malik looked at Donovan.

Donovan raised his finger, about to say something, before turning and darting to the corner. The sound of his retching echoed in the lobby. When he was done spitting out the rest of his vomit, he returned to Malik.

"Sorry." Donovan still looked queasy. Malik shook his head.

"Nah, man. All good. I just... Do we run? Upstairs to get a vantage point? I doubt this is gonna hold that guy for long."

As if on cue, there was a slam against the front doors. Liv shrieked. The desk skidded towards Malik and Donovan, who both shoved it back against the doors.

"You've seen the blueprints of this place right?" Donovan spoke hurriedly. "Is there a back way out?"

Malik shook his head.

"No. They wanted to make sure everyone got funneled in and out through the front doors."

Another slam.

Another shriek from Liv.

Another rebarracading of the door by Malik and Donovan.

"Up then?" Donovan asked, looking at the ceiling. "Plan a route to the cars?"

"It's something," Malik conceded. "Let's just stick together." Donovan nodded. They turned their attention to the women. "We're going to go upstairs," he decided, taking the charge. "Get a view of the cars and plan our escape. Where's Kelly?"

Anya and Aubrey, who had both been attempting to calm Liv, looked at each other and then quickly around them. Kelly was nowhere in sight.

"Shit!" Anya cursed, frustrated. "I took my eyes off her for one second."

"It's not your fault, but we gotta go." Malik ushered them towards the stairs.

They hurried as fast as they could up the stairs, Malik leading the way, followed by Aubrey and Anya who were practically pulling Liv with them. Donovan brought up the rear. Once upstairs, they moved in the general direction of where the cars were parked, hoping they would find a window with a clear view.

It was a struggle to move both safely, and quickly and quietly. The light from their flashlights and cell phones helped a bit, but it was still difficult to see. They checked periodically for the miracle of cell service, but it was a futile wish.

They finally found a room within line of sight of the vehicles.

"Shit." Malik hissed through gritted teeth.

Malik, Donovan, and Aubrey stood at the window. Even from this distance they could see that the windows of the cars had been smashed and the hoods popped open.

"Guarantee he fucked up the cars. Damn it!" Malik balled up a fist, but restrained from punching the wall in front of him.

"Well, there goes that idea." Donovan sighed.

"Do we just run into the woods then?" Aubrey suggested. "Lose him in there, and hope we eventually hit civilization?"

"Not sure what else. But it's gonna be hard with her." Malik nodded towards Liv. Anya held Liv and looked at the other three, at a loss as to what to do.

A click and hum made the group flinch. Suddenly there was dim, flickering emanating from the few working and sporadically installed fluorescent bulbs.

"What the hell?" Aubrey exclaimed.

"He's got a fucking generator hooked up to this place?" Donovan looked around, shaking his head.

"That's not good. Easier to see, but harder to hide." Malik rubbed his forehead.

"We should move then," Aubrey suggested. "If he just turned on a generator, he might be far away from us."

"As good a theory as any." Donovan nodded in agreement with Aubrey's plan.

"Let's go then." Malik nodded towards the door.

Aubrey helped Anya with Liv while Malik and Donovan checked outside the room for any sign of their stalker.

They heard doors slamming and movement coming from somewhere opposite of the stairs.

"Let's go," Malik whispered intensely.

They rushed to the stairs and descended as fast as possible. They saw the open front doors ahead of them. Once they hit the lobby floor, a short sprint would get them outside.

They had reached the final few steps when the figure stepped out in front of them.

Malik slipped and fell back hard on the stairs. Donovan grabbed him and pulled him up and back.

"Back upstairs! Back upstairs!" Donovan shouted.

They sprinted back up. Malik and Donovan pushed the women ahead of them. Aubrey looked back for just a moment. The figure had begun his assent up the stairs. Slowly. Methodically. In no hurry, but somehow keeping pace with them.

"Keep going up!" Malik shouted. "Third floor!"

They hooked around and continued up. Aubrey could hardly breathe. Her heart felt like it was going to rip apart. She felt lightheaded from fear and adrenaline.

"Left!" Malik shouted directions again once they hit the third floor.

They ran further.

"Right! Turn right!"

After turning the corner, Aubrey could see a set of open double doors. Partially visible under the grime and flickering lights, a sign read "THERAPY" above the doors. She looked back again. The figure was still too close. They weren't going to make it. She made brief eye contact with Donovan, whose face showed he thought the same.

"Keep going," He said, mostly to Malik. Donovan suddenly pivoted, charging back at the figure.

"No!" Aubrey shouted.

Malik put his arms out and corralled the three women past the doors while Donovan lowered his shoulder and barreled into the figure.

The figure stumbled back, but he had his hands on Donovan. He spun Donovan around and threw him to the ground. With his back to the remaining four, he pulled out the long silver instrument, knelt, and brought it down into the side of Donovan's stomach.

"Donovan!" Aubrey screamed.

The figure looked back, stood, and began to stride towards them. The horrific mask disappeared from view as Malik slammed the doors shut and slid the locks into place.

"Keep moving!" Malik waved them on. Aubrey hesitated as she stared at the closed doors. Malik grabbed her shoulders, not unkindly, but firmly. "Aubrey. We have to keep going," he told her. His eyes darted back and forth. His jaw locked. He was clearly shaken at witnessing the murder of his friend.

Aubrey nodded. They ran farther into the therapy wing.

After a while they slowed their pace, out of breath. When the deafening sounds of their own heartbeats and rushing blood subsided from their ears, they listened closely for any evidence of pursuit.

They heard nothing beyond their own breathing and the hum of the sputtering fluorescent lights.

The group stepped into the closest room to rest for a moment and formulate a plan. The room had several rotten adjustable beds. Leather wrist and ankle cuffs were still attached. Aubrey didn't want to even consider what kind of "therapy" was applied to the patients brought in here.

"Oh shit." Malk jumped back from the center of the room.

The floor had partially given way under his foot. After closer inspection, Aubrey could see extensive rot from water damage on the walls and floor. She guessed it was like this everywhere on the top floor. Decades of exposure to the elements would have taken a serious toll on the integrity of the building.

"How do we get out of here?" Aubrey turned to Malik.

"I... I don't know." Malik shook his head and started pacing.

"Malik, honey," Anya said gently. She sat against a wall with Liv, simultaneously trying to comfort Liv and reassure Malik. "You've studied these blueprints how many times? There's got to be something."

Malik shook his head.

"They built this place to ensure no one could even accidentally escape." Malik had his hands behind his head. "I mean... Shit." He stopped pacing. "It's super dangerous, but maybe we could..." His voice trailed off.

“We could do what?” Anya urged him to finish his thought.

“If we could find a rotted out, collapsed floor, we might be able to slide or lower ourselves down to the second floor and work our way out.”

“Sounds better than waiting for that... monster... to find us,” Anya encouraged the plan.

“Okay. Alright.” Malik nodded several times as he amped himself up. “So do we split up, or?”

“Are you fucking crazy?” Aubrey said, a little harsher than she meant to. “We stick together.”

“Right. Not thinking clearly.”

With that, the four began their search for a way out. They went room to room in hopes of finding an already broken through floor. If need be, they’d smash one out themselves, but they hoped to avoid creating that much noise.

They approached a room with signage for “HYDROTHERAPY.” Aubrey gasped and flinched. Under the flickering lights, inside one of the hydrotherapy boxes, was Kelly. Only her head was visible. Her eyes were closed as if asleep.

“Kelly?” Aubrey whispered.

No response.

Aubrey cautiously stepped into the room.

“Be careful,” Anya whispered. Aubrey nodded and checked all the corners of the room before she walked in.

Hesitant step after hesitant step brought Aubrey in front of the therapy box that held Kelly. She reached out a shaking hand to touch Kelly’s face.

Kelly’s decapitated head, which had been carefully balanced on her body, rolled down and hit the floor.

Aubrey stumbled backwards, both hands covering her mouth to stifle her scream. The shock, fear, horror, and adrenaline finally caught up with her. She vomited.

Aubrey wiped her mouth and worked to regain as much of her composure as she could. She returned to the others, her face tear stained and puffy.

“Let’s go,” She mumbled as she pushed past Malik.

They inspected a few more rooms. Anya continued to help Liv shuffle along. Aubrey took note of one room where the floor was extremely rotted and unstable, though not fully exposed in the way they were looking for.

A few rooms later they paused, taking a moment to clear their heads and to try to stave off the ever growing frustration. Liv sank down next to the doorway. Malik crouched against the left wall, hands braced on his knees.

"This is going to take forever," He complained. He stood up and leaned back against the wall. He tapped the back of his head against the wall and closed his eyes. "This place is massive, and we aren't covering much ground."

"Maybe we will have to split up." Anya sounded defeated. Malik nodded sadly and shrugged.

"What? No!" Aubrey wasn't going to accept that as an option.

Malik opened his eyes and threw up his hands. "What else are we going to-"

He was cut off as the figure's arm smashed through the rotted wall behind Malik and grabbed him, pulling him back into the adjoining room. The wall crumbled further as Malik was dragged through.

"Malik!" Anya screamed and rushed at the figure.

"Anya! No!" Aubrey reached a hand out to grab Anya but missed.

The figure grabbed Anya by the throat and threw her effortlessly into the adjoining room to join Malik. He turned to Aubrey. As soon as the figure took a step towards her, Aubrey turned and ran to grab Liv, who was wide-eyed and breathing rapidly. Aubrey pulled her to her feet.

"Let's go!" Aubrey shouted at Liv.

Liv's eyes focused just enough on Aubrey to show she understood.

They ran.

Liv stumbled and skidded as Aubrey practically pulled her along.

A plan formulated in Aubrey's mind as she heard the screams and howls from Malik and Anya in the distance behind her. She led Liv into the room with the unstable floor and guided her around to the far side opposite the doorway. She sat Liv down against the wall, brushing away some of the hair that was matted against Liv's face from her tears and sweat.

"Wait here," Aubrey told her.

Liv nodded weakly. Her shoulders slumped. Her head tilted slightly to her right, and she gazed off into nothing. Her breathing had calmed some, but was still shallow.

Aubrey tested the rotting floor with her foot, pushing carefully to weaken it further. Once satisfied, she wheeled one of the adjustable beds in the room over to a spot out of sight from the doorway. She squatted and waited.

She felt a little shitty about using Liv as bait, but she wasn't sure what else to do. Running wasn't working. Maybe she could kill, or at least injure the figure enough so they could get away.

Malik and Anya's wails stopped. Aubrey assumed the worst.

Heavy footsteps soon approached from down the hall. She heard them stop outside the doorway, then enter the room. Aubrey could now see clearly that the instrument this monster was using to kill her friends was a silver orbitoclast. He took a few steps forward, then hesitated. An agonizing moment later, he took one more step forward.

Aubrey rammed the bed forward into the figure's back as hard as she could.

The figure fell forward, the impact cracking almost all the way through the floor. Aubrey screamed as she exerted every last bit of her strength to lift the bed up and over so it fell onto the killer.

"Die, you fucking bastard!"

It was enough.

The floor gave way and the figure fell through. Aubrey heard the satisfying thud of the figure hitting the floor below and the crash of the bed as it followed.

She stepped back to regain her balance, having nearly fallen through herself. She looked down at the unmoving body below her. Aubrey moved around the hole and helped Liv to her feet. They stumbled back to the entrance of the therapy wing. Aubrey unlocked the doors and gripped the handles but hesitated. She took a deep breath and prepared herself to see Donovan's body before she pulled the doors open.

The hall was empty.

There were streaks of blood, and signs that someone had been dragged elsewhere.

She didn't want to think about what the figure had done to Donovan.

Aubrey walked Liv down the stairs as fast as she dared, keeping her arm around Liv's shoulders. Eventually they made it down both flights of stairs, through the lobby, and out into the night.

"We're almost there, Liv." Aubrey whispered. "Be strong for me, okay?"

Liv nodded, but didn't speak. The color had not yet returned to her skin. Her breathing seemed more regular now at least.

Aubrey had never been more grateful to see the stars and breathe fresh air, but she didn't stop. She wanted to put as much distance between them and this place as soon as possible. They crossed the yard to where they had originally entered. Aubrey gently helped push Liv through the gap in the fence first before she started to squeeze through. As she shimmied through, Aubrey glanced back at Elmhurst Asylum.

Her heart sank. What little joy she had allowed herself to feel at their escape disappeared.

The masked figure strode towards them. Not running, but rapidly closing the distance between them.

"No. No. No." Her shoulders slumped. Her breathing bordered on sobs. "No."

Her eyebrows pulled down and together. Her lips narrowed. Her nostrils flared. Aubrey pushed the rest of the way through the fence. She grabbed Liv and they ran into the woods.

Aubrey could hear the heavy steps fading away behind them, but she didn't risk looking back. Stumbling now would be a death sentence. She could feel Liv was quickly losing pace and slowed enough to turn and encourage her to keep going, but instead Aubrey halted, gasped, and covered her mouth.

Liv turned to see what Aubrey had seen.

"No, don't!" Aubrey tried to stop her from looking.

It was too late. Liv stared at Mike's lifeless body. An orbitoclast had been impaled through his eye, staking him to a tree.

Liv didn't make a sound.

Aubrey carefully approached Liv and reached out to touch her shoulder.

"Liv?" Aubrey spoke softly.

"No!" Liv shrieked, and smacked Aubrey's hand away. She started to back away from Aubrey.

"Liv, please," Aubrey pleaded. "Don't leave me. We can get out of here."

Liv shook her head over and over again. Laughter and strange sobs emitted from deep inside her. Her arms shook as she waved her hands to tell Aubrey to stay away, and she soon disappeared into the darkness.

A crunch of leaves and snap of a twig brought Aubrey back from the haze of despair she was in.

The masked figure approached.

Aubrey turned and ran again. Her legs and lungs burned. She felt the sting of branches striking against her skin as she sprinted past. She held her arms up to protect her face and eyes, preventing her from seeing as she ran headfirst into something tall and solid. Her head rocked back from the impact.

Not something. Someone.

She screamed and swung her arms out in defense. The person grunted.

"Hey! It's me! It's me!" a familiar voice pierced through the rushing sound in her ears.

"Donovan?" Aubrey's mouth hung open. She stared at him, then threw her arms around him.

"Ow! Shit," he complained.

She pulled back. Donovan gripped his side and winced. His shirt was bloody from where he had been stabbed.

"I'm sorry!" Aubrey brought one hand to her mouth and raised the other, palm out, in apology. Donovan shook his head.

"It's alright." He grimaced.

"How did you..." Her eyes scanned him, not quite believing he was there.

"I dunno." Donovan scrunched his face as he tried to remember. "I guess he thought I was already dead or I'd bleed out after he dragged me off. Or he was more interested in the ones that had gotten away." He paused. "Anyone else?"

Aubrey opened her mouth to respond, but the words stuck in her throat. She shook her head, and forced back her tears. Donovan nodded somberly.

"I think I found a way out of here." He indicated somewhere behind him with a nod. "But we definitely shouldn't stand around here too long."

Aubrey nodded and followed close.

"What did you find?" Aubrey whispered.

"It's an old storage shed thing." Donvan winced, his breathing shaky. "There's a dock, and I think I saw a rowboat. If it's not seaworthy, we can at least maybe walk and follow the water back to civilization."

Aubrey watched Donovan limp as they moved along.

"This way," he said.

Aubrey followed. She tried to keep the images of what she had witnessed at bay. She looked around into the woods, afraid they'd be accosted by the masked figure at any moment. Her eyes settled back on Donovan who, though he walked in pain, led her on with confidence. She thought it a little strange, that he seemed to know where he was going. She figured Donovan had a good memory and sense of direction.

"There it is," he announced.

A fairly large structure stood before them. The front was more shed-like, but it was attached to a larger metal structure behind it. It reminded Aubrey of a turtle in a way. A wire fence ran out and back from the sides of the building, which made the only viable way to the back through the front door.

Donovan approached the door and opened it.

"Come on," he said softly, a small but comforting smile on his face. He gestured to the doorway with his head and stepped inside.

She followed. Donovan had turned on an electric lantern and continued to walk towards the back. Aubrey looked around the now illuminated room. A clothing rack held greyish-blue jumpsuits hung from hangers. On a table, neatly stacked, were tanned, dried flesh colored masks. They were featureless, save the silvery studs on the mouth and eyes. Next to the masks were silvery hammers and orbitoclasts. Barbaric tools for lobotomies.

Aubrey stopped. New confusion and fear washed over her.

"Donovan?" She barely whispered.

He continued to shuffle away.

"Donovan?" Aubrey spoke with more volume and conviction. "Please stop."

He did.

"Turn around. Please."

Donovan did so.

Aubrey forced her legs to move forward. She stopped in front of Donovan, reached out, and slowly moved his hand away from his wound. With her other hand she spread the tear in his shirt wider so she could see where he had been stabbed.

The wound looked more like a cut than a puncture. Deep enough to bleed, but not nearly severe enough to cause real injury. It had already been stitched up. Donovan winced as Aubrey put pressure on the wound with her fingers. She shook her head and stepped back by the table.

"What is this?" Her voice cracked. She picked up a mask and shook it at Donovan. "Some kind of joke? All fake?"

"No." Donovan winced at Aubrey's question. "Not a joke at all. And not fake... Orchestrated."

Aubrey shook her head.

"Explain it to me," Aubrey demanded. "All of it." Aubrey squared her jaw and pointed at nothing in particular.

Donovan nodded and paused for a moment. He took a deep breath through his nose and released it out of his pursed lips.

"My grandfather worked here as an orderly, a long time ago."

"The photograph..."

Donovan nodded.

"Exactly. An oversight that we left it, but we didn't want to disturb the asylum too much. Would be too obvious that there was something being set up. Lucky for me, Brennon was the one that found it. Easy to discredit any thought he had... But, yeah. My grandfather saw all the abuse and neglect that happened here. For all the reasons you theorized. He and a few others did what they could, but they had no real power to do anything. Once Elmhurst was shut down, he moved on to other careers, but still saw the same dehumanizing attitude society had taken. He wanted to change it, but didn't know how. He passed on that philosophy, mission, or whatever you want to call it, to his son, my father, and they continued looking for a way to fix the rot they saw. But in order to do that, they needed to find the cause."

"And what was it?" Aubrey, though incredulous, was genuinely curious.

"Lack of fear. True primal fear. The fear of and respect for what lurks out in the darkness. The fear that kept our ancestors alive. Held tribes together. Gave them a reason to protect each other. Society has become too comfortable. Without that fear... Without that respect of what dwells in the deep, deep dark, we've turned on each other. Squabble over petty differences. Ignore the things that are good and true and pure. Once they realized that, a plan took form. A plan that I elevated, and then we put into action."

"So we were all puppets in your plan then?"

"What? No. Not at all. Puppet would imply an indifference from me, and no free will from all of you. You weren't puppets, but each of you had a role to play."

Aubrey waited for Donovan to continue.

"Brennon, Mike, and Kelly. Their own indifference and lack of empathy sealed their fates. They were... sacrifices, if you will. The ones that were punished for their sins. Liv..." Some signs of remorse crossed Donovan's face. "She was a wildcard. Her actions tonight would determine what happened to her. I had no idea that her mind was so... fragile. She's suffered enough. We'll make sure she makes it out safely. Malik and Anya... Hurt and, unfortunately, traumatized, but we need Malik to spread the story, and Anya will push him to do so."

"They're alive?" Aubrey let a brief smile of joy through.

"Yes. We were careful to make sure they weren't killed. They didn't deserve it. And, like I said, we need them."

Aubrey raised her hand to stop Donovan. She closed her eyes and shook her head.

"You keep saying 'we.' Who is 'we?'"

"My brothers and I."

"Brothers? Like a cult?"

Donovan laughed.

"No. No. Nothing like that. My actual, physical brothers. It's how the 'masked madman' seemed to be everywhere at once. Why we heard him behind us even when he was at the bottom of the stairs. Why you saw a figure of the same relative height and body type pursuing you, even after you killed him."

"He did die? One of your brothers, I mean."

"Yes. But, we all knew the risks of this going in. And it proved me right about you."

"You said we all had a role in this. What was... is... mine?"

Donovan took a deep breath.

"In our quest to be the authors of new urban legends, the architects of new reasons to be home before sundown, we needed a leader. I happened to be more creative than my brothers, so I was chosen to be that leader. The new father, if you will. And I... " Donovan hesitated. "I want you to be the new mother."

"What?" Aubrey pressed her fingertips against her forehead and looked down.

"Please. Hear me out. You've shown that you are strong and resourceful. You've shown empathy, but still a willingness to kill to protect. I know you don't like to speak of it much, but I know what you've been through. I see the darkness and creativity in your art and in your eyes. You could help us, help me, unleash our darkness to change things around us."

Donovan turned around so his back was to Aubrey and took a few steps towards the back door.

"Some of my brothers are waiting on the other side of that door to take us away from here and to our next plan. I... would really like you to join us."

A whirlwind of thoughts rushed through Aubrey's mind. Things she had tried to bury deep and forget. Feelings of fear, anger, hope, joy, despair, and resolve, all muddled her thoughts. She stared at the back of Donovan's head. She reached out, and picked up a hammer from the table.

Donovan raised his head slightly when he heard the scraping sound of the hammer being picked up from the table, but he did not turn around.

"I won't try to stop you, Aubrey." He spoke softly and calmly, a hint of sadness in his voice. "And I promise you there won't be any attempts at revenge. My brothers will just move on to the next phase without me. I knew this was a possible outcome. This was my risk to take. I… I just ask that you truly consider what I've said. That's all. The choice here is yours."

Aubrey willed herself forward. She approached Donovan, who didn't turn around. She slipped the fingers of her left hand between the fingers of his right. He cocked his head and looked at her.

She looked up at him. Her eyes glistened from the tears that had formed. Her lips twitched, fighting between a smile or frown.

"Okay?" Donovan asked softly, his eyes scanned her face.

Aubrey managed a smile, and nodded her head in resolve.

"Okay," she answered. Donovan smiled kindly.

Hand in hand, the two walked forward, passed through the now open door, and into the new darkness.

REST STOP

BY JOSHUA MAHN

I looked down the barrel

---

of my secondhand .38 special and wished, not for the first time, that I'd saved a round for myself.

I've been inside of this gas station for, near as I can reckon, a few hours by now. I don't think I'll get out.

~~

I'd been visiting with a few buddies of mine up in the panhandle. We got a cabin, caught up, drank up, and gave each other hard times for most of a weekend. When it came time to head back, I played the fool and insisted I could make the drive in one go, despite how late it had gotten on this moonless night.

So I drove.

The night was dark and so was my coffee. When the latter failed, the former pressed on with all its might. My truck's broken clock flickered nonsensical runes at me through the miles of the late night and early morning. The radio occasionally coughed up pieces of country-fried white noise for me from the foggy aether.

These rural Floridian highways are notorious for their monotony, deeper than any other. As the thicketed and swampy miles bled out from under me, my eyelids grew dangerously heavy. I was brought to the precipice of sleep and delirium, my thoughts abstract and inexplicable. Curious and surreal. A smell was a memory, which became a notion, which became a recursive, fractal thought, and so on. I was practically dreaming behind the wheel. Though I was stone sober, I was really in no shape to be driving.

~~

The lurch from a pothole jarred me back to the moment. I shook myself and realized that I didn't recognize any of the road around me. I must have missed my turn.

I cursed myself out rather thoroughly and pulled my phone out to set the GPS. Of course there was no signal at all back here amidst these swamps and hollers.

Fuming, I peeled off the road at the nearest exit I could find, groggy and anxious to be home once more. My truck coasted smoothly into the soupy fog of the lowland road, ungraced by street lights or other travellers. Somewhere on my way I must have finally crossed that invisible and dangerous threshold into slumber.

~~

I awoke to the crunching of gravel beneath my tires.

My truck was gently coasting toward some two-bit, rundown gas station. The needle on the gauge pointed sullenly to "E".

How long had I been asleep? How long had my truck coasted without me? I could have sworn I had at least half a tank left.

Fear and relief washed over my confusion. Fool that I was, I counted my blessings! I felt relief that I had ended up here instead of wrapped around a tree, or stuck in the front grate of some tractor trailer. I even felt lucky. Not only had I survived falling asleep at the wheel for some unknown amount of time, but I had somehow rolled safe and sound, exactly where I needed to be!

What were the odds?

I even promised myself I'd start praying more often.

I took a deep breath. I went to check my phone to see how long I had been out, or if I could find any signal, but the damn thing was completely dead.

Shit.

As glad as I was to be alive, I was still stranded who-knows-where in the middle of the night. Turning on the weak and yellowish console light, I reached into the glovebox for the old revolver my folks had gotten me ages ago. I stuffed it into my waistband. I was probably being paranoid. Still, if it came to it, what couldn't I solve with five rounds?

~~~

The gravel threatened to punch through the thin soles of my shoes. The old lights flickered above the station's only two pumps, filthy with dust.

Dozens of moths beat themselves into a frenzy against the bulbs above, killing themselves to seek the warmth they thought they needed.

My eyes traced the front of the grimy store, and it had all the accoutrements of any backwoods station. Cords of firewood stacked up for sale. A crooked sign advertising boiled peanuts. C-list cigarettes for rock bottom prices. Live bait.

The plate glass windows were smudged with handprints, and though I could see nobody inside, a little placard hung jauntily enough.

Open! Come on in.

So I let myself in.
~~~

Goddamnit. Why did I do that?

~~~

The bells on the door jingled weakly.

"Hello?" I called out.

Nearly all the lights were on, though some seemed to be barely clinging to life. Dirty slushy machines spun lazily. The fridges stood tall with their bounty of sodas and beers. The place smelled like old meat, or roadkill.

Whatever. I just needed to get in and get out.

I tried calling out again, hoping that somebody would manifest, to no avail. My confusion deepened. Had the attendant simply left the store abandoned for the night without locking up?

I shook my head and rubbed my eyes, too sleepy and confused to make heads or tails of it. I decided I'd just walk back to my truck and doze until morning.

I was about to step through the door when the hair on my arm prickled. My blood chilled within my veins.

The light was on inside my truck. Someone was sitting in the driver's seat, staring straight at me. I'm pretty sure they were smiling.

~~~

Goosebumps prickled over every inch of my flesh. I reached for the reassuring weight of my revolver. I called out uselessly for a vanished attendant, just as a lamb bleats for a ram when it smells a wolf.

Nobody answered.

I took a few steps back from the door, suddenly feeling vulnerable with my back unprotected, and shifted towards the checkout counter. I'd taken my eyes off of the truck for hardly a second before I heard the door slam shut.

The truck was empty now.

Hadn't I locked the door? I couldn't even remember. The console light cast its feeble yellow glow into the uninhabited cab for a few seconds longer, then extinguished itself.

I kept my back to the counter and clutched the revolver in my waistband tighter. I yelled out into the dark, hoping whoever it was could hear me in the parking lot.

> ***"I shook my head and rubbed my eyes, too sleepy and confused to make heads or tails of it, I determined I'd walk back to my truck and doze until morning.***

"That's not your truck! There's nothing worth stealing in there! Just go away and we'll pretend nothing happened!"

I had always hoped to sound brave in a time of danger, but where I wish my voice had boomed, it cracked. A cruel reminder that I was small, afraid, and helpless rippled through my body. My stomach danced and my breathing hitched. I grit my teeth and stared out into the foggy night. I hoped to see the other person. I hoped to never see them again.

I noticed silence. When was the last time a gas station was completely, utterly silent?

God, I was so tired.

~~~
~~~

At last I saw movement.

A silhouette manifested at the barest fringes of light outside. I knew it had to be whoever had been in my truck. My instincts screamed it at me, but my muscles were locked in place. I let loose a river of fearful and hateful words at them, despite the windows and distance between us.

As the figure stepped further into the light, their form solidified into a distinct body. I could get a good look at last. I truly wish I hadn't. Disbelief and disgust wrapped like fingers around my throat as I was forced by the unrelenting reality of the situation to look on.

It walked with a strange, rolling stride. Like its legs weren't the right length, somehow. It was stark nude. Its body… malformed. I call it an "it" because I must. Everything about it was unnatural. Its belly distended like a starving captive's. Its pale skin shone like that of a damp maggot. Its neck stretched nearly a foot past its slumped shoulders, though it was absurdly thin, like a child's wrist.

Worst of all, though, was its face. Deepset eyes stared at me, relentless in their gaze. Its mouth was puckered and leechlike, caked in dried blood. I could see sharp teeth at the gates of a mouth crammed absolutely full of bloody flesh. Even through the door I could hear it making strange noises. Something between gurgling and choking. How could it eat anything with a throat like that?

But something about it felt familiar.

Yes, as it shambled closer I could see now. Those miserable eyes shone clearer and I understood. They were exactly like my own. Exactly. It was as if a corrupted copy of myself had been made in some unknown celestial workshop and set loose.

As I watched, frozen, it completed its journey to the store's door, mere feet away. It stared at me, and I stared at it.

I screamed.

It screamed too. It matched my pitch and volume with a manipulation of its lips. I took it to be a smile.

I stumbled backwards. My blood felt curdled and thick. The monster danced backwards in a pantomime of me, flailing its arms as I had done. I gasped for breath, like a fish left in the sand, and leapt towards the door, thinking to lock it. But as I reached for the door, so too did the creature.

I drew my hand back in shock, afraid of what would become all too real if it touched the door as well.

The flimsy sign on the door flapped gently, mocking me.

Closed, it chided.

We stared at each other for a moment. Then, the thing smiled widely at me. Small bits of gore dribbled out of its mouth onto its belly. It hissed with what I can only assume was humor.

My only protection was the unlocked glass door. It was so close to me now. Why wasn't it coming in? Was it toying with me?

"Stop," I begged.

"*Stop*," it rasped, blood and saliva leaking from its lips, to its naked belly, and to the gravel below.

"Leave me alone!"

"*Leave me alone!*" Blood spritzed across the window as it raised its voice.

My blood warmed, then boiled. I drew out my revolver, cocked the hammer, and leveled it at the creature's chest.

Time seemed to slow. My pulse thumped in my ears. Then, quiet.

It took a rattling breath. Then it pointed a long, scraggly, willow branch of a finger at me. Its filthy and cracked nail pointed at my heart, just as I aimed my gun at its own.

"*Oot, oot, oot!*" it rasped. It was smiling. It was laughing at me!

I pulled the trigger.

The gunshot roared through the small space and rattled my skull as the tempered-glass panel of the door shattered onto the ground in thousands of shards and a cloud of dust.

"*Oot! Oot! Oot!*" it howled with excited laughter. It was clapping its hands.

I pulled the trigger four more times, letting each round burrow into the entity's center mass from fewer than five feet away.

My ears rang. The gunshots danced across my corneas in the low light. A tendril of consciousness slowly returned to me.

"*Oot, oot, oot...*" The chuckles continued.

It stood tall. As proud as could be. It seemed unharmed. Its scraggly finger was pointing at the sign which spun lazily between us, goading and reprimanding in equal measure.

Open! Come on in. - Closed. - Open! Come on in. - Closed.

The carousel of permissions whirled on.

I trembled as it watched me. A sheen of sweat clung to me like cobwebs as my adrenaline began to taper off. My throat was closing in. My stomach gurgled.

It moved again.

Gravel crunched beneath its bare feet as it stepped towards the unshattered window to my left. It stared at me, and the sounds of sucking and choking burbled up, louder than before. It put a finger into its puckered mouth, and sucked it, then delicately touched the window where it began to smear with its mixture of blood and saliva.

Fridge.

My muscles tensed. My eyes locked upon its own. My own.

Casually, thoughtfully, it returned its gnarled fingertip to its mouth, inking the horrid pen. Beneath the first message, it drew a smiley face.

I made some sort of noise, I'm sure, but it only tutted gently at me now.

"*Oot, oot, oot.*"

Gravel crunched again. It turned without further spectacle and walked, as slowly as it pleased, back to my truck, opened the door, and sat down. From the driver's seat it stared at me, unwaveringly. I was nearly paralyzed with fear, watching it in return.

We looked at each other for some time. Its leechlike mouth wrought into a false smile cast in the dim yellow, until at last the console light flickered to sleep.

I sat and listened for more noise, and heard nothing. Not even crickets. But I stared on. I knew it was still staring at me. I knew this night would never end.

I looked down the barrel of my secondhand .38 special. I took a deep breath. What else could I do?

I turned slowly, as if it would make any difference, and made my way towards the wall of refrigerators. Beside them, a door dusted with fog beckoned me. What had been uninteresting before now filled me with profound and significant dread.

I considered stepping outside. Trying to run. But where could I possibly go? How could I slip away while this creature guarded the only exit?

I took a rattling breath, the oxygen goopy and heavy in my chest, and touched the chilly door. It was unlocked, sinking back beneath my touch. I crossed the threshold.

~~

The stench of rot smashed into me. I gagged. Oily, sweet, wretched. Decomposition.

My teeth clattered against each other as I stepped around a tower of beer cases, my fingers locked with dread around my revolver and growing colder by the moment. The space was diamond hazy, but I found what it wanted me to.

Slumped against the far wall of the fridge was a corpse, tinted green and blue with decay. Its belly was swollen and distended from the gasses of decomposition.

I inched closer. I had to.

When I saw that the corpse was my own, I vomited.

~~

Gasping, sobbing in a way I did not comprehend, I forced myself to look on.

Its clothes were my own. The very same I wore now. Its face, though pallid and stiffened, was certainly my own. I touched it, felt the cool, unyielding skin. Its left hand was wrenched in a display of agony, but the right hand was clenched into a fist, clutching something close.

I wrung the rigid and mortised fingers open, with considerable effort, and the prize spilled out, clattering onto the concrete floor below.

A single .38 special round.

One more shot.

~~

The bells on the front door jingled weakly somewhere behind me, and I could hear that terrible laugh once more as I loaded the last round into the cylinder.

"*Oot, oot, oot!*"

A COFFEE SANCTUARY
LOST AND FOUND

BY LISA BUI

April 11, 2021. A Sunday night.

The night of my coffee bar evaluation. The shop had been rearranged into stations where the new hires would each be tested on different materials now that the months of training were over. While waiting for my turn at the espresso station, I happened to glance at the bold AXUM sign at the front of the shop. Axum, a homely neighborhood coffee located in the heart of Winter Garden, popular for its coffee drinks as well as other crafted beverages. I remembered thinking to myself how estranged I felt the first time I walked into the shop for my interview, and yet somehow – in that exact same time and space – it was also my new home. I'd moved around so much but never felt entirely like I belonged anywhere until I came to Axum. Anticipation boiled inside me, creating a chain of knots from my tummy to my throat where it tightened and left my voice hoarse, as if I'd been stranded in the desert for hours. For a short second that seemed like an eternity, my whole body was shaken with an electrifying sensation, striking up a question that was really more of a realization: "Why did it take me so long to make it home?"

The coffee house culture has been around since approximately the 15th century and was brought to popularity worldwide through the growth of cross-continental trade. The first coffee shop ever to be established is believed to have been at a "Kiva Han" under the Ottoman Empire. With time, coffee houses gradually started gaining political importance due to their accessibility and popularity as places for debates. In fact, they were remarkably imperative meeting places and were often referred to as public sanctuaries for one's repressed states of mind. I myself was born into a repressive culture. Growing up, I was never encouraged to freely express my emotions. A lesson that I've carried well into my adulthood. Coffee houses were the only sanctuaries that allowed me a place to stream my thoughts to a blog platform. In the comfort of public anonymity provided by the coffee shop, my unresolved emotions found their catharsis in the rhythmic comings and goings of people, chattering background noises, the chocolaty smell occasionally blended with a lavender-scented candle, and a playlist of random songs that somehow met me in the middle and coaxed my emotions to the surface. I had grown up drinking coffee as a "ritual", but unexpectedly, it was the coffee houses that helped shape who I am today.

I'm here for various reasons, many of which I see reflected in the reasons coffee and coffee houses exist. In Columbia, they "granted artists, journalists, and writers equity to the property, some doubling as galleries and convention centers"1. In France, "Parisian cafes were hotbeds for thought, philosophy, and art, attracting the likes of Jean Cocteau, Ernest Hemingway, and F. Scott Fitzgerald"1. Meanwhile, in America, "'coffee houses were points of planning protests during the Vietnam War, a process later deemed "G.I. Cafes.'"1. In the Middle East and West Asia, various coffee shops offer shisha - flavored tobacco smoked through a hookah - to customers alongside their drink selections. And in Vietnam, visiting coffee houses is an integral part of people's daily routines. Italy cannot be forgotten either, due to its brilliant invention of the espresso bar, which paved the way for many modern espresso-based drinks. With the progression of society, coffee houses have introduced Wifi hot-spots, allowing people to congregate, talk, read, write, entertain, or simply pass time, solidifying them as cultural standpoints. Coffee houses laid the groundwork for various activists, intellectuals, and artists to meet and connect. That a cup of coffee could bridge the intellectual and physical gap that might have otherwise divided people from various social standings was a profound example of art and beauty.

I am someone who yearns to speak up, someone who desperately wants to express, and someone who genuinely desires to connect to and empower the "silent ones." I've come to understand that I belong not to any national culture, but to the coffee culture itself. Growing up without much of a voice, my comfort zone was within my thoughts where I could snuggle into myself and my introverted world. I dreaded having to interact with people at first, not knowing that my soul had actually been craving that connection all these years. The coffee shop was no longer just my introspective sanctuary, it also became my playground. A place where I can be my authentic self and have fun at the same time. I found myself returning to the coffee shop, to my "natural habitat", where my true values, characteristics, and personality had the chance to be the most genuine. I wanted to be there so much that I worked to find every possible way to stream my shortcomings into passion and hope. I never before expected that crafting amazing coffee beverages and making my guests happy would enrich my life the way it has. It brings me endless joy to see my usual customers and ask them about their days, even though sometimes these are just brief exchanges of greetings or short updates on life. Here, I have learned to be patient and observe people while putting my own life in perspective. Here, I make progress in the formation of my own self through blog posts, projects, and study. Here, I find solace in being surrounded by people and yet still "safeguarded" within my own world, where my reality aligns with others. Here, I learn about making coffee. Here, I've found the concept of a true "home"within the world and within myself. Where I feel loved and find belonging even though I'm not perfect. And finally, here, my passion is reaffirmed and instilled with grace, hope, support, and inspiration from the numerous wonderful people I've crossed paths with. Colleagues, friends, customers- both happy and unhappy- and family. And to think it all started with the simple desire to express one's introspective outlook about life. Coffee houses were once many people's refuge and they continue to be even now, including mine. It starts from the farms, then travels across the oceans, then arrives at different places, with a whole team of people ready to craft the final product. Coffee is teamwork, connection, love, and dedication all in one. It takes so much time, labor, and effort to go from coffee bean to beverage. It is a work of progress that its beauty can be shared globally. And, at this exact moment I am part of the history that coffee ever was and will be...

I've made it 9,659 miles across the globe, far from my origin and beginning, only to have found the true home I've been searching for my whole life. It isn't an exact location nor time, but rather through every part of my journey, it has always been within me. With the onset of my quarter-life crisis, I've been stricken with a realization that I'm not yet whole. Rather, I am becoming. I'm both a complete revision and a work in progress. Keeping this thought in mind alleviates my doubts about my identity. Like a pour-over, it started as a thought, just a few drips at first, and needed time to bloom. Then a repetition, rounds and rounds of affirmations and support that I poured into my life and passion. And then finally, a mindset. A Full cup. Bold but flavorful. Where each sip is a different flavor that assures myself more than ever of one thing: Coffee is my slow-burned love narrative. What's even better? I can pour it differently every time. If I ever decide it doesn't taste right, there's always a chance for new flavors. There's always time for a new cup..

"ACCEPT THAT YOU ARE A WORK IN PROGRESS, BOTH A REVISION AND A DRAFT: YOU ARE BETTER AND MORE COMPLETE THAN EARLIER VERSIONS OF YOURSELF, BUT YOU ALSO HAVE WORK TO DO. BE OPEN TO CHANGE. ALLOW YOURSELF TO BE REVISED. KEEP MOVING." – Maggie Smith

WHO SHE WAS

BY EMERALD MARTINEZ

PROLOGUE

"Dad, come on!" I shouted from down on our front lawn. I kept my hands folded tight under my arms in attempt to keep warm. "Would you just let me do it?"

My father, crawling on his knees across our roof, waved his arm out in dismissal.

"I'm handling this, Eva! Just tell me if it's straight!"

I looked up to where he was stringing a line of white icicle lights across the edge of our second story roof, squinting my eyes against the sun that did little to warm me in the chill November air.

"You're too old to be doing this!" I taunted. I bit my cheek to keep from laughing as he scooted a foot at a time along the shingles.

"I'm not letting you up here, Eva! You'll fall and break your neck!"

A string of lights wrapped around his foot. He shook his foot out to loosen them, losing his balance in the process. He fell backwards on the roof, landing on his back and sliding a few inches towards the edge. He wedged his foot against the rain gutter. The aluminum creaked as water and leaves sloshed down onto the front lawn. I jumped back to avoid the splash.

"You're the one who's gonna fall!"

"Oh ye of little faith. Let me handle this, Eva. I know what I'm doing." He connected the last few white wire strings before climbing down the metal ladder.

"Welcome back to earth," I teased. He knocked me in the shoulder as he came to stand by me.

"Quiet you," he said, turning to face the house. "How's it look?"

"Fine, now. We'll have to see it when it gets dark." My father grunted an agreement. “Okay now the tree!” I said, clapping my hands together.

“Give a man a minute, would you?” he groaned, reaching around himself to massage his sore back. “Let’s have some dinner first.”

“Fine,” I mumbled.

“Chinese?” he asked. I nodded. “Alright, I’ll run out and pick some up. You get the ornaments out while I’m gone.”

“Okay.”

He checked his pockets for his keys and wallet, nodding to himself when he confirmed he had both, and walked to the car.

“You know,” I called out to him. “I could run out and pick up the food. Just toss me the keys. You should go inside and take a load off,” I skipped forward, holding my hands out.

He laughed, holding his keys away from me.

“Not a chance, kid. You know the deal.”

“But I-”

“When you’re eighteen we’ll see about you driving. Until then,” he gestured to the empty crates that held the outdoor Christmas lights. “You stay here.”

Decorating the Christmas tree was my favorite part of the Christmas preparation process. While my father forbade me from climbing around on the roof, the tree was my domain. He would sit back in his chair, perusing his paperwork and periodically peering over his glasses to critique my work. I would sneer at him and continue on. It was the most enjoyable few hours of the holiday. Just me and my dad.

I stood in our living room facing the naked tree, tapping my socked foot against the beige carpet. Deciding I might as well get everything ready, I walked over to the door in the kitchen that opened to the garage, which was mostly used as a storage facility. I dug through a pile of boxes and crates, holding my breath against the clouds of dust that rose off the cardboard surfaces.

I found the box of Christmas lights and hoisted it up onto my hip so I could carry it into the living room, where I dropped it onto the floor. The lights inside were white, just like the ones strung up outside. I unwound the string of lights and stretched them across the floor so I would be able to see each of the light bulbs. I plugged them into the outlet to test them. Two of the three strands lit up like little stars across the carpet. The third strands remained dim.

I picked the strand up and checked each bulb. Around the middle I found the wire had been worn down, the rubber casing rubbed away to expose fraying wires.

"Oh come on," I mumbled. The faulty strand of lights was throwing a wrench in my favorite holiday tradition.

I checked my watch. My father would be home soon and I wanted to have everything ready before he was back with dinner.

I returned to the garage to search for extra lights. Finding none, my attention turned to the attic.

The pull down ladder into the attic was located in the ceiling of my father's closet. If anything were needed from it my father would insist on getting it himself. He never liked me in his room.

Well, my father wasn't home and this was an emergency. We needed lights, and if I couldn't find any I would have to call him before he got home so he could pick some up. I was on a time sensitive mission. It had to qualify as an exception.

The attic was even dustier than the garage. Just a few moments after pulling myself through the hatch I inhaled a thick cloud that tasted of sawdust and deprived my mouth of moisture. I stuck my head back through the hatch and coughed, taking a few clean breaths before returning to the attic. I inhaled more cautiously after that.

Many of the boxes in the attic had labels that indicated their lack of use, such as "Baby Clothes" and "Cassette Tapes." I sat on the edge of the hatch, dangling my legs into my father's closet, and reached around the attic. I shifted the boxes left and right, checking each label.

I finally found a promising label. A plastic crate with a sticker labeled, "Extra X-Mas Stuff" was tucked farther back in the crawlspace. I stretched out my arm, reaching for the black plastic handle on the side of the crate. It was just out of my reach. I stretched a little father, straining my back to wrap my fingers around the handle. I pulled the crate towards me with some difficulty. A heavy cardboard box sat on top of the crate, weighing it down.

I sighed and pulled myself fully into the attic, keeping my head down and crawling closed to the box. I grabbed the crate with both hands and yanked it closer.

The box on top of the crate shifted with the movement, sliding off the top of the crate and toppling over. It's contents spilled across the rough wooden boards.

"Damn it," I hissed, crawling closer. I righted the box and started to scoop up the contents back into their home. It appeared to be just a bunch of photographs. They had spilled facedown. I picked up a stack and flipped them over.

In the quiet attic, my intake of breath seemed thunderous.

> ***"I held a hand against my stomach. A lurching feeling turned my organs, like that first drop on a roller coaster after having just gotten used to the upward climb.***

A woman with a delicate, heart shaped face smiled up at me from the photograph. She sat on my beige couch, the same one in the living room downstairs. Her bare feet were pulled up with toes painted a dark blue. Her curly blonde hair fell in a mess around her face, a few ringlets hanging in front of her jade eyes. Her cheeks dimpled deeply as she looked into the camera. It was the most beautiful face I had ever seen, and I knew it all too well.

It was the first time I had seen my mother's face in almost ten years.

It was the same face that hovered over my sleeping, eight-year-old form. She had shaken me gently. I remember her full lips moving. She was speaking to me. At almost eighteen I still could not remember what she had said. It didn't matter. The next morning, she was gone.

I thought I heard someone knocking. I soon realized it was only my heart hammering in my chest.

Overcome by a sort of frenzy, I grabbed another handful of pictures. In each of them I found more of her. I found her laughing, making kissing faces, twirling in a flowing blue dress, and even sleeping. I found her standing next to my father and posed next to his sister, who wore a nasty scowl.

"Mom," I whispered.

I didn't want to look at the photographs. I knew I shouldn't. My mother had left us. It had been so long ago. It didn't matter anymore. My father and I had a life, one that she had chosen not to be a part of. In the ten years she had been gone she hadn't tried to reach out to my father, or me not even once. Not even during the holidays.

I dropped the photographs back into the box with trembling hands. Beads of sweat had formed on my forehead from the warmth of the insulated crawl space. I wiped them away with the back of my hand.

Almost all the photographs had been replaced when I found a thick stack of purple envelopes of varying shades, kept together with a thick rubber band. I would have tossed it into the box along with the photographs. The sight of my own name written in a delicate script across the front stopped me.

I pulled the rubber band off the envelopes, wincing in pain when it snapped against my knuckles. My name and address were written across every single envelope. I opened the top one and removed a photograph of a window that looked out over a large grassy lawn. Three large sunflowers partially blocked the view, framed by the purple painted window.

I flipped the photograph over. A note was written in the same smooth script.

To my beautiful daughter on her seventeenth birthday,

It breaks my heart I cannot be with you today. You're getting so big now, and I've missed it all. These sunflowers are my favorite, and they make me think of you. I hope that one day you'll come see them for yourself.

Have a wonderful day, and think of me when you blow out your candles. I wish I was there with you.

Happy Birthday,

Love Mom.

I held a hand against my stomach. A lurching feeling turned my organs, like that first drop on a roller coaster after having just gotten used to the upward climb.

I flipped the envelope over. In the upper left hand corner *Dinah King* was written above an address in Blue Ridge, only a couple hours away from my home in Atlanta.

My father rarely spoke of my mother. On the few occasions he did, he told me he had no idea where she was and that it didn't matter because wherever she was, she wasn't thinking of us. The seventeen envelopes I held in my hands proved that that wasn't the case.

I heard a distant slam from downstairs.

"Eva!" my father called. "Dinner's here!"

I jumped, throwing the envelopes into the box and shoving it back behind a stack of crates. I grabbed a string of lights from the Extra X-Mas box and dropped back down into my father's closet, landing wrong on my foot. A twinge of pain shot through my ankle. I ignored it and pushed the ladder back through the hatch.

I ran downstairs, jumping the last three steps of the stairs.

"Eva?" came my father's voice from the kitchen.

"Yeah!" I replied, putting my hand on my chest to try and slow my breathing. I threw the lights into the living room and ran into the kitchen, rounding the corner a little too fast.

"Woah, slow down, I'll wait for you," he said, pulling off his coat. He looked up at me and frowned. A furrow formed between his eyebrows. "Eva?"

"Yes?" I asked. My voice sounded squeaky to my own ears.

My father stepped forward, reaching out his hand. He put it on top of my head and ran his thumb over my forehead.

"You're all sweaty. Are you okay?"

I heard my heart slamming away again. I prayed he could not hear it, too.

"Yeah. I'm fine," I lied. "It's just- I just dragged a box in from the garage. It was heavy."

"Hm," he mumbled. His eyes narrowed. "Alright."

I couldn't enjoy decorating the tree. My thoughts kept returning to the bundle of hidden birthday cards in the attic. I stood behind the pine, wrapping a string of white lights through its branches. My fingers were sticky with the fragrant sap.

I peered through the needles at my father. He sat in his usual chair, holding a stack of papers in one hand and an egg roll in the other. He was the same man that had raised me and yet something about him seemed so foreign to me.

"Dad?" I asked, still hiding behind the tree. I made a show of fluffing the branches.

"Hm?"

"Can I ask you something?"

"Sure," he said, not taking his eyes off the papers.

"Do you know where mom is?"

He looked up from the papers, turning his gaze on me. I ducked behind the tree.

"Why do you ask?"

"I was just wondering. It's Christmas, you know?"

"I suppose..."

It was silent for a few moments. I held my breath, unwilling to press the subject but praying for an answer.

"No. I don't. You know that," he finally responded.

"I know. I just wondered if things had changed, maybe." I moved to the other side of the tree, pulling the lights with me. "Does she ever call?"

"Jesus, Eva," he groaned, pulling his glasses off and tossing them onto the coffee table. "What is this? Why the sudden curiosity?"

I didn't face him. I kept my focus on the lights, taking one bulb between my fingers and unscrewing it, then screwing it back in, watching as the lights of that strand dimmed and lit up again.

"I was just wondering, you know? Maybe because it's Christmas, or maybe because I'm almost eighteen. Did she ever try and contact us again, after she..." I trailed off.

"No. She never did."

A lie.

"And you don't know where she went?" I asked.

"No. I don't."

Another lie.

"Okay."

I looked to the beige couch and thought of the photograph of my mother sitting there. After ten years without her, the thought of her dwelling in this house ceased to be anything more than just a daydream. The photograph had made her former residence real.

I looked around the house, void of any trace of her, and yet everything looked different.

"Alright," my father said, standing up from his chair and clapping his hands together. "Sun's down. Let's see how those lights turned out."

We pulled our sweaters on and walked outside. The cold air shoved through the front door and scraped across my cheeks.

We stood in the middle of the lawn and faced our house. Perfectly straight lines of twinkling white lights outlined the house, casting a soft light over the lawn and surrounding trees.

I crossed my arms and looked down our street. Half a dozen other houses had also put up their Christmas lights. All of them were colorful. Cheerful, fluorescent shades of green, blue, red, and yellow illuminated the houses in a cozy glow. I couldn't help but think those houses looked more like Christmas than ours. I had never noticed how plain our house with it's white lights seemed in comparison.

"Dad?"

"Hm?"

"Why don't we use colored lights?" I asked, turning my eyes back to our perfectly lined home.

"They're so childish, don't you think?" he said, looking with disdain at the other houses. "White is clean. It's simple." He held his hands up to frame our house. "Simple is better." He nodded in satisfaction at his work and patted my shoulder. "Let's get inside. It's cold out here," he said, and started walking back to the house.

I stayed outside a bit longer, staring at the lights until they blurred into bright white starbursts. When I shut my eyes, red spots splashed across the back of my eyelids.

I opened my eyes again and pulled a deep buried memory from the back of my mind. I had been standing here with my mom, holding her hand as we looked up at the same white lights.

I couldn't remember more than that, but something told me that she would have preferred colored lights.

One

The attic stunk of the thick and musty scent of old, decaying wood. It coated the inside of my nostrils when I inhaled. Summer had arrived and with it, the heat. Trapped inside the timber chamber, it permeated my clothes, sinking into my skin, and made me sweat. The attic, barely large enough to call it so, was the most uncomfortable place I could imagine. It was not at all some place to sit and relax, but it was the only place I could see my mother.

I sat hunched over in the cramped space, keeping my head low to avoid banging it on the sloped roof. Sweat dripped down the back of my neck, soaking loose strands of my hair. I sat cross-legged, the unfinished wood splintering into my legs, with a box of photos on my lap.

I had lost track of how many times I climbed into the attic since Christmas. I also lost count of how many times I searched in vain for photographs of my mother and I together. In all the polaroids and glossy faced images, only my mother or my parents together could be seen. No trace of me, their child, could be found. It often felt like I was looking in on a different family to which I didn't belong; one that held no room for a third person. Could my arrival have made the house too crowded for my mother?

No. She didn't leave because of me. The birthday cards proved that much. She missed me, she said as much in the note on the sunflower photograph card.

Had my father done something?

The morning after my mother left, I'd found my father sitting in the kitchen. His wide hands covered his face. His shoulders hunched low over the table, forming a shell around himself.

"Daddy?" I had said. The house felt cold that morning. The white tiles chilled the bottoms of my little feet as I approached him. "Daddy where's mommy?" She hadn't woken me up that morning.

My father lowered his hands to the table then, his movements so slow that not even the softest *thump* could be heard when the backs of his hands fell onto the wood.

"She's gone, Eva."

"Well when is she coming back? She wouldn't go on an adventure without me."

"She didn't go on any adventure."

"Well then where is she?" I felt a real but inexplicable fear crawl into my stomach.

"I don't know, Eva. But she isn't coming back." He lifted his gaze from his hands, resting his eyes on a spot above my head. I remember feeling angry that he didn't look at me. "She isn't coming back," he said again. "It's just you and me now."

I know I must have launched into a fit of questions followed by hysterics. I know I must have cried or screamed or done any of the things a normal eight-year-old girl would have done at being told that her mother was never going to come back to her. I can't remember that part though. I just remember the defeat on his face as he told me that I had been abandoned.

Had it been defeat? Or was it guilt for whatever he had done that drove my mother away? Perhaps it was the knowledge that he would henceforth bar his own daughter from speaking to her mother.

I held the picture of her sitting on the couch in my fingers, careful only to touch the edges to prevent smudging. I wondered whose couch she was sitting on now.

My phone, balanced on one of the boxes beside me, chimed out an alarm, alerting me to my father's incoming arrival. I held the photograph once more, touching my fingertip to her face in farewell.

"Bye mom," I whispered, putting her back in the box and climbing down the rickety ladder into my father's closet.

My father returned home from work at half after six, just as he did every day. He was a man that thought of schedules as rituals, believing that with everything planned there would be no surprises and therefore, peace.

He walked into the kitchen just as I placed frozen lasagna in the oven.

"Hey Dad," I said, kissing his cheek and taking his briefcase from him. He mumbled a returned greeting and sat at the table, loosening his tie. When he looked up at me he tilted his head to the side.

"Your face is red. Are you hot?" he asked. I wiped the sweat from my forehead, still feeling the effects of sitting in the attic.

"I went for a walk outside," I lied. "Hot day today."

His eyes narrowed for a moment, but then he nodded, accepting my fib. It wasn't a complete lie. It was July in Atlanta. Every day was a hot day.

I couldn't tell him about the photographs. When my mother left us he had stripped the house of her presence. Every picture, article of clothing, or personal item that she left behind was shoved into those boxes and hidden away where he believed I wouldn't find them. Now that I had, they were my secret. I would never risk him permanently removing them from my reach.

With my mother gone from his life, my father threw himself into mine. He was involved in every aspect of my life, from my failed little league attempts right up to my clubs in high school. Every decision was a decision made together. Unfortunately, we had finally reached a decision that we didn't agree on.

"Dad I wanted to talk to you about something," I started.

He sat back in his seat, his head tilted back, resting on the back of the chair. He closed his eyes, massaging his temples.

"It's about college," I continued.

"Hm?" he mumbled. "What about it?"

"I've just been thinking-"

"Could you get me some iced tea, Eva?" he interrupted. I sighed, but stood up.

"Of course," I obeyed. I pulled the plastic blue pitcher from the fridge, pouring him a glass before sitting back down. He opened his eyes and sat up, reaching for the glass. "Anyway," I began again, eager to return to the discussion. "about college."

"What about it?"

"I've been thinking lately and-" I struggled to remember the well thought out speech I had prepared in the bathroom mirror this morning. It had been something about love and loyalty and hasty decisions, but I couldn't seem to remember it. My father stared at me, waiting. I felt the pressure of his gaze and my own fear of the effect my words could have.

"Dad I don't want to go away for college, I want to stay here," I told him.

He straightened in his chair. His bushy brown eyebrows drew together. His frown deepened the wrinkles forming around his mouth.

"That isn't what we discussed, Eva," he responded.

"I know that! And believe me I've been giving this a lot of thought and-"

"A lot of thought? Of course you haven't! We've been planning this for over a year now. Have you given it as much thought as that?"

"Well no but-"

"Alright then. We've already decided that you'll go out of state for college; it's only a matter of where. We can make a final decision when you get your acceptance letters. You have sent in your applications haven't you?"

"Not yet but Dad, listen-"

"Eva, you can't be serious? I gave you those brochures weeks ago!"

"Dad, the applications aren't even due until October."

"I don't care! You need to get them in now, show some initiative. You want to study management after all. Show you have solid organization skills."

"Dad, I don't know for sure if that's what I want. That's what I'm trying to talk to you about."

My father pinched the bridge of his nose, shutting his eyes to me.

"Eva, this makes no sense. We had a plan."

"I know, but Dad I just think it would be better for me to go to school locally. Maybe take some more time to figure out what I want."

"We know what you want," he said, opening his eyes again. He reached a hand out to me, placing it on my arm. "Are you nervous? Are you afraid you won't be accepted? Eva with your record any college would be lucky to have you."

"That's not it," I said, feeling my argument slipping away from me.

"Then what? Going out of state will be good for you."

"But don't you want me to stay close?" I pleaded, leaning closer. My father sighed, taking my hands in his.

"Of course I do. But I want what's best for you, and what's best for you is to go out of state. I know this, and you do too. You're just nervous. You've been homeschooled for so long, I know going outside that seems like a lot. But I know it's the best thing for you."

He smiled with the minimal, slight upturn of the corners of his mouth that was almost unnoticeable to most. I knew he had decided, and therefore so did I.

I nodded.

"Yeah, okay, Dad. Sure," I agreed. He lifted his hand and patted the top of my head.

"Good girl," he praised. "Now, where do you want to go to dinner for your birthday tomorrow?"

"I don't have a preference. Anywhere you want."

Growing up, I couldn't help but feel a sense of obligation towards my father. My mother's leaving had broken his heart. I knew that, although I also knew he would never admit it.

The photographs in the attic changed things. My father, once my shield of protection from all things toxic, now appeared to be the source of obstruction from the truth.

I sat at the desk in my room. A number of college websites painted my computer screen, waiting for my attention. I couldn't give it to them. Every time I tried to start an application I couldn't get past entering my name.

Instead I sat in the rolling chair, my legs pulled up underneath me, holding one of the envelopes from the attic that contained a birthday card. I stroked a thumb over the return address in Blue Ridge. Each envelope had the same one. My mother must be there.

I would never be able to make that drive once I left for college. I would be out of state and out of range. If I could convince my father to support my choice to go to school locally, then I would be eighteen with my own car and able to make the drive. I would be able to see her. I would be able to ask her the questions I had.

"Why did you leave?" I would ask her. "Why didn't you take me with you?"

Would she recognize me? Had she seen me at all since she left? Did my father at least send her photographs of me growing up? Or did he rob her entirely of her right to me? If he did, why didn't she fight for me?

I ran through the pieces of my plan in my head, chewing my thumb nail, when my bedroom door swung open. I jumped, almost losing my balance on the chair, and spun around, tucking the envelope underneath me.

"Just came in to say goodnight," he said, crossing his arms. "How are the applications coming?"

"Oh, um," I struggled to catch my mind up to the situation. I couldn't think of anything to say quick enough, so I just pointed to the computer screen. "They're coming," I said.

He narrowed his eyes at the screen.

"Hm," he mumbled. "Alright. Well goodnight."

After he left I released the breath I held and removed the envelope, flattening it out on my desk with both hands before I tucked it into the back of a desk drawer.

I sighed, then stood up, crossing my room to climb in between the slate colored sheets of my bed. I reached over to turn the lamp off. All light left my room except for the beaming strip below my door. I waited. I heard the sounds of my father's footsteps thumping through the silent house. The red lights of my alarm clock read 9:26. At that moment I knew he was laying out his shirt and pants for the next day before brushing his teeth in preparation for bed.

At 9:30 I heard his socked footsteps padding on the polished wood of the hallway. They paused. The strip of light disappeared. His footsteps retreated to his room, followed by the click of his door shutting.

I waited an additional few minutes before reaching through the dark, feeling around for the knob on my bedside table drawer. I pulled it open, searching blindly inside the drawer. In the dark recesses my hand closed around a small tube. I withdrew my hand under the covers, pulling the blankets over my head. I flipped the top of the tube open, holding it to my nose.

The healing scent of lavender and peppermint filled my senses. I inhaled deeply, shutting my eyes to allow the memory of my mother a clear path to front of my mind. The hand lotion was another treasure I uncovered from the depths of the attic's secrets. I'd found a half empty and expired bottle in the boxes and I recognized it instantly. My mother, unlike my father, didn't hold to specific routines. She was playful and spontaneous, deciding on a whim to take me along on some adventure to a flea market or even, on a day off from school, to some cattle show. There was one thing that remained constant with my mother. Her scent. Lavender and peppermint perfumed every memory of her. I wasted no time in tracking the brand down to purchase my own supply.

I squeezed a small amount of lotion from the tube onto my wrist, an action I rarely did for fear that my father would recognize the smell. I decided to allow myself the small birthday present.

I reached out from under my covers to replace the tube of lotion in my drawer, pushing it towards the back. I curled up with my knees to my chest, placing my hand under my head to allow me to breathe in my mother, letting her memory soothe me to sleep.

"Come to me, Eva!"

I heard my mother's whisper clearer than any alarm. I hadn't opened my eyes yet, but I felt the hand against my cheek. I could smell her there, sitting beside me, holding my face as she called me to awareness.

Every morning when I was a child, my mother would tiptoe into my room. She'd open the blinds, letting the sun in to greet me, and sit on the edge of my bed, running her fingers through my chestnut curls. She would be the first thing I saw. My mother woke me up every morning.

Until the one morning she didn't.

On the morning I turned eighteen I was sure I would open my eyes to her face again. But before I knew it the dream slipped away from me. It wasn't my mother, but my own hand that held my face.

I sat up in bed, holding my wrist to my nose so I could smell her one more time before washing the lotion off in the bathroom before breakfast.

"Well good morning there, birthday girl!" my father exclaimed when I walked into the kitchen. He patted my shoulder, giving me a quick kiss on the top of my head.

"Thanks Dad," I said, moving to retrieve a mug and pour myself some coffee.

"You shouldn't drink that sewage," he told me. I shook my head.

"I need it. There are worse habits in the world." I set down the mug before hoisting myself onto the marble countertop, reclaiming the coffee in both of my hands. I swung my feet beneath me, bouncing my heels off the dark cherry cabinets.

"That is true," he conceded, pulling his reading glasses from his shirt pocket and placing them on his nose. In his hands he held a stack of mail, including a few brightly colored envelopes.

"Looks like you got a few birthday cards," he observed, pulling the envelopes from the stack.

"Oh lovely. Let me guess," I held up my hand and began to count on my fingers. "Your secretaries, my virtual school advisor, and Aunt Lola."

"Hm," he grumbled, allowing a small smirk to acknowledge my correct guesses.

My birthday had never been much of a big event. I hadn't attended public school since the third grade. Virtual school wasn't exactly a watering hole of social interaction. My circle consisted entirely of my father's associates and their kids, my advisor, and my father's very old and very bitter spinster sister Lola.

He handed me each of the cards one by one, pausing at a lilac colored envelope. He frowned, flipping the envelope to look at both sides. His nostrils flared when he exhaled. He folded the envelope; contents still sealed inside, and stuffed it into his trouser pockets.

I recognized it at once. There was a stack just like it in the attic and one hidden in my desk at this very moment. My mother had sent me another card. Another photograph with a loving note to me on the back.

"Was that for me?" I asked, trying not to sound accusatory.

"What?" he asked, looking up at me. I nodded towards his pocket.

"The card. Mine?" I asked again. I hoped my efforts to keep my teeth from locking together weren't as obvious as they felt.

He shook his head so tightly the loosening skin under his chin trembled with the movement.

"No. Just something for me."

"Dad, it's a colorful envelope. That screams birthday card. As far as I'm aware I'm the only one celebrating another year closer to death. Just give it to me," I said, reaching my hand out.

"I said no!" he snapped. I withdrew my hand, wrapping it around my coffee mug and gripping tightly to keep myself from lunging for the purple treasure. My father shook his head and smiled. "Really, it's probably a thank you card from one of the new men. I just hired someone to help me manage the new offices. He was really grateful for the opportunity," he explained. I narrowed my eyes. My father was not one for lengthy explanations.

"Right," I said. *Liar.*

He busied his hands with the rest of the mail, checking each envelope with extra attention, no doubt ensuring no other traces of my mother managed to interlope. He tossed them aside when he finished.

"Anyway, I thought Italian for your birthday dinner. Is that alright?" he asked, changing the subject.

My thoughts were still on the confiscated card in his pocket.

"Yeah. Of course."

"That waiter was incompetent!" my father complained, stomping through our front door. He'd butted heads with the inflamed acne-faced teen that waited on us at the restaurant. The first incident had been an honest mistake about a diet soda, but my father's scolding had put the boy on edge, making him clumsy.

"He was nervous," I observed, walking into the kitchen and placing the present from my father on the table. I had hoped to open the small parcel to find a set of car keys, only to discover a wad of gift cards and a clinking gold charm bracelet that one of his secretaries probably selected. The disappointment left a bitter taste in my mouth as if I was holding the desired car key on my tongue, made worse by his thievery of my card. No matter. I would steal it from the attic tomorrow.

"I don't care how nervous he was. He should have been doing his job."

"You scared him!" I defended the stranger.

"Scared him? What does he have to be scared of! He works a menial job; it's not rocket science. It's laziness and lack of focus." He walked over to the counter and dropped his keys in a white ceramic bowl. The blinking light of the answering machine waited.

"You didn't have to be that hard on him. I'm sure it's not as easy as it looks," I said. "Not that you would know..." I added under my breath.

My father waved his hand in dismissal.

"Nonsense. You just don't understand what it is to have a job."

"That's because you won't let me have one!" I mumbled, busying myself with the ribbon from the present. My father's head whipped to the side to glare at me, his mouth slightly agape.

"You're being awfully rude tonight, Eva," he said in a flat-toned warning.

I held my breath for a moment, biting back another retort. He continued to watch me as if he were waiting for me to explain myself.

"I take you out for a nice dinner, buy you a lovely gift, and you've had a bad attitude all night. Sit down, we need to have a discussion." He pointed to the chair beside me. I glanced to my right, measuring the distance between the stairs and myself. "Don't even think about it," he warned, catching my gaze.

I sighed, yanking the chair away from the table so it squealed loudly against the tiles. My father glared at me again but didn't say anything. I sat back and crossed my arms.

He pressed the button beside the flashing red light on the answering machine. The machine beeped and replayed a message from one of his associates. Another beep sounded and Aunt Lola's wheezing voice shrieked through the cold kitchen.

"*Michael! It's your baby sister, Lola,*" she began, followed by a serious of hacking coughs. "*Tell the kid I said happy birthday!*" Another stream of coughs. "*And call me back, I need to ask you a legal question. Some little shit keeps letting his dog shit on my lawn. I want to know if I can sue and get the rat confiscated.*"

"Old hag," I muttered. My father shot me another, increasingly threatening, glare. "What?" I defended, throwing my hands up. "You're not even a lawyer!"

He shook his head and turned his attention back to the machine. It beeped, signaling the start of a new message, but no voice came through.

"What's this?" my father mumbled, his thick finger hovering over the delete button. "Some crank caller."

"*Michael?*" A soft, hesitant voice finally sounded. "*Michael, are you there?*"

"What in God's name-" my father said through gritted teeth. I leaned forward to try and hear the quiet voice better.

"*Michael, it's me. I know I shouldn't be calling but I just want to talk to her.*" A knot formed in my stomach. I knew that voice.

Come to me, Eva.

I leaned even farther in my chair, resisting the urge to vault across the room.

"*It's her birthday and-*"

"Message deleted," came the robotic voice of the machine, cutting off the musical voice.

"No!" I screamed, launching from my chair across the room, reaching for the machine. My father's solid arm swung out, wrapping around my torso to prevent me from reaching the machine.

"That was her!" I shrieked, stumbling back. The edge of the sink bumped into my lower back. "It was her! I know it was her! How could you do that?" I cried.

My father did not look at me. His face was flushed an angry red.

"You don't know what you're talking about," he said, his teeth still ground together.

"You're lying! I know you're lying!" I felt the tears burning through my tear ducts. "That was her! I know it was her! You're lying to me! I know that card was from her too!" He angled his face even farther away from me. "It was!" I shouted. "It was and you lied! All you do is lie to me! She knows I'm here! That's why you want me to leave! You-"

"Enough!" he barked, halting the next stream of screams in my throat.

He'd never yelled at me before.

"I do everything for you, Eva! So shut your mouth and show me some respect!" He held his finger to my face, the same finger he'd used to erase my mother from the machine. "You do not get an opinion on how I parent you! You are a child, Eva! Start acting like it! Now get upstairs! We're done with this!"

"But-" I began, my voice much smaller than it had been a few moments ago.

His hand slammed down on the counter. The ceramic bowl with the keys jumped at the same time I did.

"Now!" He yelled. My mouth clamped down around any other words I might have said.

I retreated from the kitchen on shaking knees. On the way upstairs I gripped the stairwell tight enough to where my knuckles turned white, just trying to stay standing.

In my room I shut my door, then fell back against it, sliding down to the beige carpet. I folded my legs into my chest, resting my forehead against my knees. The tears, subdued before by the shock of my father's outburst, escaped. They dripped down my nose and onto my jeans, leaving a damp spot.

I knew my father had been withholding information about my mother from me. That much had been obvious, what with the attic filled with confiscated pictures. At that moment I knew for certain that he was hiding more than just a broken heart from me.

My mother had called. She had our phone number. She knew I was still here.

I know I shouldn't be calling...

My suspicions that my father must have forbidden her from talking to me were confirmed, but why did he do it? Could whatever she had done been so horrible that my father would feel it necessary to bar her from me? When I thought of my mother all I could remember was her gentle disposition, or her playful smile, and most of all the light that seemed to surround her always. I couldn't imagine someone so good doing anything so bad. He had to have been the guilty party.

I sat against my door for a while. I'm not sure how long. When I stopped crying I uncurled myself from the floor, peeled my clothes off, and slipped between the covers of my bed.

One revelation stood out to me more than any other. It drew my thoughts to an address hidden in my desk. It hardened my resolve to find the woman whose voice still haunted my dreams.

"Soon," I whispered into the darkness. "I promise, I'm coming soon."

Two

The next week passed in tense silence and a succession of wary glances. I didn't bring up my mother's call. He didn't bring up the college applications that he, no doubt, wished would take me far away from where she was. He was giving me my space, but I knew it was only a matter of time.

A line had been drawn in the sand with my father and all of his secrets on one side, and my mother and I on the other. At least that's what I believed.

The possibility that I actually stood on that side alone never occurred to me.

The newspaper lay open on the kitchen table when I came down for breakfast on the sixth morning of our Cold War. I glanced at the paper in passing. My eyes paused on a black and white photograph of a grinning woman with a delicate round face. Soft blonde curls framed her cheeks. For a moment I couldn't believe it. My mother smiled up from the page.

I glanced at my father. He hadn't noticed my entrance. He stood with his back to me at the stove, cooking his usual breakfast of a single fried egg with two sausage links. I picked up the paper.

Former Savannah resident Dinah King, 37, Died August 8th, 2015 in Blue Ridge, GA.

Her family will hold her memorial service on Sunday morning, August 13th, at the local church. All friends and family are welcome to attend to pay respects and say goodbye to this remarkable woman and mother.

I froze. My chest felt tight. I held the newspaper with trembling hands. I had been so close. A year of studying her face. A year of waiting to turn eighteen. A year of dreaming, planning my questions for her, and falling asleep to the smell of her lotion. All of it for nothing. It couldn't be right. That wasn't how things were supposed to happen. I found it difficult to inhale.

I didn't realize how long I held the paper until it was snatched from my hand. Shreds of grainy gray paper tore off in between my clutched fingers. I jumped. My father stood before me. He held the crumpled paper in one fist and a plate of eggs and toast in the other.

"Eat," he commanded, putting the plate down on the table.

"Dad, what-" I started.

"I said, eat."

He turned away, crumpling the paper into a tight packed ball before dropping it into the trash. My throat felt tight. My eyes burned.

"She's dead?" I asked. He nodded.

"I'm sorry, Eva. I meant to throw out the paper before you came down."

I reached out to clutch the table, dropping into the chair. My father said nothing. He only watched me. He crossed his arms over his chest.

"How?" I managed to ask, looking up at him. He shook his head.

"You don't need to know that," he said, sitting across from me with his own breakfast.

"Dad. Please?" I pleaded. "She was my mom."

"No," he snapped. "No she wasn't. And Eva, I really don't think-"

"Please?"

He stared at me for a moment, his jaw clenched. Finally, he sighed.

"She drowned herself."

My stomach lurched. All my fantasies of a reunion, dashed to pieces. Smudged out by a single paragraph of black ink.

My father cleared his throat and began to eat. His fork clinked against the plate. I watched him for a few minutes, searching for any sign to show me that he had been affected by my mother's passing. Puffiness around the eyes or a slight tremble in his usually steady hand. I found nothing. He ate his breakfast as he did every morning at nine while reading the local news. His world remained the same. A horrible thought occurred to me.

"Did you do it on purpose?" I spoke. My words sounded more like a shaky breath than anything else. They scratched my dry throat on their way out.

My father continued to chew, looking down at the runny yellow yoke that spilled from his fried egg.

"The paper," I clarified, my voice more solid. "Did you leave it out on purpose?"

He looked up at that. His bushy eyebrows shooting up towards his hairline, finally showing some sort of reaction.

"Eva how could you think that?" He didn't sound angry. He was surprised. Surprised that I would believe it? Or surprised that I figured it out?

"You hid her from me for years! Every birthday card, every phone call, every picture you've managed to take! And the *one* thing you finally let slip is that my mom is *dead*?" I rose up from my chair, slamming my hip on the table. I ignored the bruising impact, though it shook the surface and nearly spilled his coffee.

"You're upset. I understand. But you're being ridiculous," he defended. He raised his hands up, pleading not guilty.

"Am I?"

"Eva, I wouldn't do that to you. I am just as shocked as you are. I didn't want you to find out like that. Sit down,"

I wanted to step away. To back out of the kitchen, run upstairs, and smell her lotion so I could maybe, just maybe, pretend she was still out there to be found.

"Eva," my father called to me, his voice level like one speaking to a strange, unpredictable animal that's crossed their path. "Sit down."

The strength given to me by my anger left me. My knees shook. I collapsed back into the seat. Whether from shock or obedience, I couldn't be sure.

"Hurry up and eat," he ordered, pointing his fork at my plate. "You need to get back on your college applications."

Upstairs in my room my mind spun. I tugged at my hair. I bit down on my lip, refusing to cry. My mother died. My father hadn't been planning to tell me.

My mother died.

My mom was dead and he had just gone to work like any other weekday.

He said he didn't mean to leave the newspaper out. He seemed to be telling the truth. He said he was going to tell me about it later. But was he? If I hadn't come into the kitchen when I did it might have been too late. The newspaper might have ended up in the trash without me seeing it. Who knows if I would have found out? He hid everything about my mother from me. Would he have gone so far as to hide her suicide?

Suicide.

The word made me cringe.

I wanted to see her. I *needed* to see her.

I ran to my father's room, jerked the ladder down in his closet and climbed up. The sticky heat of the attic hit me like a wave from an opened oven. Already I felt beads of sweat forming along my hairline.

I reached forward to the point where the edge of the attic entrance dug into my stomach. I gripped the box of pictures and pulled it over, balancing it on my shoulder as I stumbled back down the latter. My ankle gave out when I hit the carpet of the closet. I fell to the floor, the box falling with me. It landed on its side next to me. I heard the crunch of glass. One of the framed photographs must have cracked. Loose pictures spilled onto the floor.

I spread them out. Each one of them took their own space on the off-white carpet, none overlapping. I needed to see them all. I needed to see every one of my mother's smiles, smirks, and even a few of her frowns. If I didn't memorize each of these photographs, then she would be gone forever and I couldn't let that happen. She had to continue to exist somehow.

In my frenzy, I didn't hear the sound of an engine. I didn't hear the car door slam or the locking beep. My brain didn't register the front door opening and closing, or the sound of my father's footsteps on the stairs. I didn't even hear him calling my name into my empty bedroom. If I had, maybe I could have prevented his outburst.

"What are you doing?" he barked.

I froze. My hands trembled, hovering over the collage I'd made. When I looked up, my father stood framed in the doorway. He looked even larger than normal. From my spot on the floor, I was eight years old again looking up at my giant daddy whose shoulders spread across the width of the doorframe.

"How did you find these?" he demanded, gravel in his voice.

"I was just-" I glanced at the mess of pictures, albums, and frames surrounding me. "Looking for something."

"Looking for what?"

It was obvious what I was doing. But surely he understood. He had to. He was my dad and she was mom. There had to have been some room for sympathy deep beneath his anger with her.

"I just wanted a picture of her."

His nostrils flared. He held his hands in fists at his sides. His face reddened.

He stepped forward, his heavy footfalls shaking the floor. He grabbed me by the arm, his fingers digging into my muscle.

"You're hurting me!" I shouted, stumbling as he lifted me from the floor. He stepped backwards, out of the closet, dragging me with him. "Dad, stop!" I screamed. He turned and threw me back towards his bedroom door.

"Nothing has changed!" he yelled, reaching out to take hold of my chin. "Your mother is not important. She never has been. Now get back to your room! Focus on something real! College is real! This-" he pointed back towards the mess in his closet with his free hand. "Isn't real!" He released my chin.

My eyes stung. I felt the tears cut down my cheeks. My chest felt hot. I bit my lip to keep from crying out again and rubbed my sore jaw.

"I just want one!" I cried. "Why are you doing this to me? I love her! Just give me something!" I begged.

He ignored me, turning his back on me. He started to close the closet door, to block me from her.

"Please!" I screamed, lunging forward for the door.

"Eva, STOP!" he bellowed.

First I saw his arm swing out to block me. Next, I felt something solid collide with my cheekbone.

For the second time that day, my knees lost function. I crumpled to the floor, cupping my face in my hand. I didn't even cry. I just sat there, looking up at him.

My father looked almost as surprised as I was.

"Eva I-" he started, stepping forward. I flinched. He stopped.

There was that line in the sand, more prominent than ever, between us. I could almost see it.

My father straightened his back and turned away from me, opening the closet door. He collected the pictures, dropping them back into the box. I watched him in defeated silence. After a few moments, he disappeared through his bedroom door, carrying the box of what was left of my mother with him.

Whatever switch had been turned off was flicked on when I heard him leave through the front door.

My vision tunneled and seemed to throb with each heartbeat that thrummed through me. I felt my chest implode. My breath rasped from my lungs one after the other, yet I couldn't seem to bring in enough oxygen. My cheek felt tender under my fingertips.

My heart raced. I fell forward onto my father's bedroom floor, drooping until my forehead touched the carpet. Its fibers scratched at my skin at first until the tears that began to pour soaked them through.

"Mom," I whispered, without really knowing why.

WINTER BONFIRE

by Londyn Rayne

when embers rise

they harmonize with the myriad of stars

sparks blend in with the heavens

as ashes descend

like snowflakes in December

FUNCTIONAL STAIN

by Joshua Mahn

The dementia of rebirth,
Damn man, there's a coffee-breath thought
A half-remembered magnum opus and
Ghost pains from a gruesome death.
Last century's trauma stooping me lower to the ground,
My chin dragging on graveyard dirt as I try crawling backwards,
A tombstone chips my teeth.

But then
What's worse than that
Is not getting another spin on the carousel
Right?

I mean I always thought
If I
Got dementia I'd need
A .44 magnum and a
Shotglass of something
Like love
And I think
I'll think my last braincells on a dock or
In the
Woods but
What if

A little baby barely remembers and remembers less every day as
They forget they were once an old woman and
She was once sick and heartbroken and
So alone somewhere and
Somewhere
Where
Was I

Oh yes heaven
One slim door inside of a narrow
Gated community with a
Tired and underpaid guard who never could become a cop
And never could kick the
Aspartame powertrip

Lucky you were born
In just the right county of your particular country
To hear just the right gospel so you're really
Truly saved
Now smile and behave
Just right

Oh my god what if
What if they are right
Or nobody is
and there's nothing
No time to be smug
Or sad I guess but
God what are the odds
That I know everything just right

Who can put expectation like that on just one little life
Or even on a thousand
Unless
Unless...

THE HUNTRESS : BRAETHOUS

BY AARON MORRISON

"This is the Tressa IV. Requesting a docking platform."

Kyra kept her skiff circling as she waited for permission from the port of Praxia. Braethous was predominantly swampland, with tall trees and lakes stretching across the landscape as far as Kyra could see. The sky, at least where she hovered, was a deep, rich blue with streaks of green.

"Tressa IV. *Proceed to docking platform thirteen.*"

"Thank you."

Kyra steered her skiff to the platform and landed. After securing the vehicle, she registered with the harbourmaster.

"First time visiting Braethous and our fine village of Praxia?" he asked her.

Kyra had been distracted, looking at the sky.

"Hmm? Oh. Yeah. How'd you know?"

The harbourmaster laughed. "Everyone is surprised when they see the sky here. It's either that," he indicated upwards with his head, "or dark clouds with rain, which I'm sure is how you pictured it. It's usually one or the other, not much in between." The harbourmaster handed Kyra her copy of the registration. "There you go. Anything else I can help you with?"

"Where would I go for information about hunts or work?"

The harbourmaster nodded. "The village hall. Can't miss it. Magistrate Baroon or one of his assistants has all that information. The inn isn't too far from there, either."

"I appreciate your help."

The harbourmaster nodded.

Kyra followed the walkways towards the center of the village. The buildings were all on stilts to keep them elevated above the marshy ground. Praxia was built in one of the more open areas of Braethous, constructed around the population of trees. The various farms and ranches could be found on the far edges of the outskirts of Praxia. Beyond that were the swamps proper.

As the harbourmaster had said, Kyra found the village hall fairly easily. Inside, she passed a multitude of people milling about, going about their daily business. Their clothing, while predominantly browns and greens, had elements of bright blues and reds. It appeared to Kyra that while the locals kept to practical clothing, they were not without some sense of style.

"Yes! But when are you going to get this resolved? I lost another several of my gryats last night!" An older man, skin leathery from years in the sun, gestured angrily. His voice, while not fully shouting, was quite loud. He spoke to a man of similar age.

"Yoval. I understand your frustration, and I am trying to take care of it," the other man reasoned. "I am sure more people will come to hunt down whatever is doing this."

Yoval simply gestured vaguely, and shook his head in frustration.

"Yoval. Old friend. Get home to your family. I assure you, we will continue to do all we can."

The old man nodded and sighed, though his anger did not completely dissipate, and he turned to leave. As he did, he saw Kyra standing a few feet behind and eyed her garb.

"Another hunter. Maybe you can actually catch something and not run out on us like the rest." Yoval stormed past Kyra. The other man shook his head.

"I apologize for the rudeness of my friend. I promise we here in Praxia are usually more hospitable, but I must admit, these are stressful times."

"It sounds like whatever the problem is, it's getting worse. Are you Magistrate Bardon?" The man nodded.

"I am. And you are correct, uh," the Magistrate paused, not knowing her name.

"Kyra."

"Kyra. Yes. It started with some livestock being taken from four gryat farms. Some were left mutilated. We've had a few disappearances as well, which may or may not be related."

"Is there a lot of dangerous wildlife here?"

"The swamps are filled with krogalls. Make no mistake, they are deadly, but not normally as aggressive as this seems to be. So either something is happening to make them that way, one particularly nasty krogall, or some other animal entirely."

"Who's mainly being affected?"

"Give me a moment. I can show you." The magistrate turned to get a map.

Kyra looked around the hall as she waited. She noticed a group of three women to her right. Two were dressed the same, in stone colored sleeveless hooded jerkins with matching pants, and boots that went midway up their shins. Each had a bow, quiver, knife, and satchel. They looked relatively young, maybe twenty cycles, and clearly spent a good amount of time in the sun. One had long dark green hair, pulled back high in a braid. The other had short, slightly messy, gray and pink hair.

The third woman was dressed much in the same way, though there was a design stitched into her jerkin the other two did not have. She was taller than the others and had a sense of authority about her. The scars on her skin, the tone of which was the same rich dark as the night skies of Ardwin, were a record of many hunts. She appeared to have been watching Kyra, who greeted her with a quick smile before turning her attention back to the magistrate, who had returned with a map.

"So. As I was saying. You have Yoval's farm here, the Bratzl's here, and the Jorgon's here. So if you'd like to start there, you have their locations."

"You said there were four farms though."

Magistrate Bardon sighed and nodded like a guilty child.

"You're right. I did." He sighed again. "The fourth is here." He marked it on the map. "It belongs to Pabiyan, who has, well, a very different idea as to what is behind all the carnage and disappearances." Kyra waited for an explanation. The magistrate realized that Kyra wasn't going to let him get away with withholding any information. "Pabiyan seems to think there is a zhu-trask living in the swamps, which is completely outrageous."

"Why? What's a zhu-trask?"

"It's a legend. A scary story you tell around a campfire, or to make sure your children behave so they don't wander off into the swamps. As if krogalls weren't reason enough."

"Well, whatever is out there, hopefully I'll find it."

"I wish you all the luck then."

Kyra took her leave and walked back outside.

Night was starting to fall. Light flickered from the gas lanterns installed throughout the village. It was a peaceful place, but had a sense of tension in the air.

"Huntress! A moment of your time."

Kyra turned toward the voice. The woman who had been watching her followed her outside. The other two women stood a few steps behind. The woman raised her hand in greeting.

"I am Seraphina. This is Brielle." The woman with the braid bowed her head slightly. "And this is Eliana." The gray and pink haired woman did the same.

"Kyra."

"It's very nice to meet you. I apologize if approaching you like this is strange."

Kyra laughed.

"Well, we'll never meet new people if we never speak to anyone."

"Well said." Seraphina smiled. "Are you from Ultarria?"

"I am, actually." Kyra looked moderately shocked that someone could tell where she was from. "How did you know?"

"I recognized the nashorn hide in your armor. The style is very similar to what I remember other hunters having there."

"You've been there?" Seraphina nodded. Kyra was surprised again. It wasn't unheard of that her homeworld would get visitors, or that her fellow Ultarrians would travel elsewhere, but having traveled as much as she had the past few cycles she'd learned that travel and trade was much more common on other planets.

"I completed my Proving there."

Kyra had a moment of recognition.

"You are all from the Sisters of Fianna, right?"

"Yes! That's why we are here actually. Brielle and Eliana are my wards. I'm overseeing their Proving."

Night was almost fully upon the village now.

"Should we all head to the inn? We could continue our conversation there," Seraphina suggested.

"Let's go," Kyra agreed, and the four started towards the inn. "Did you come here to hunt this mystery creature?"

"Not originally. My wards chose Braethous as their hunting ground for their Proving. Just so happened there was this extra issue. A standard krogall will be enough, but if we find the one causing these problems, even better."

They entered the inn, found an open table, and sat down. They ordered a round of gryat stew and Praxian ale.

"What brought you to Braethous?" Seraphina asked between sips of the ale.

"I heard a rumor about the requested hunt. Figured a new challenge and maybe some extra coin would be nice."

Seraphina laughed at this.

"A fair reason. Have you been back to Ultarria recently?"

Kyra shook her head, careful not to betray any emotions.

"I haven't. You?"

"Not since my Proving. I would love to visit again though. Hunt the plains." Seraphine smiled with fond memory. "Do you know a huntress named Amara? She accompanied us on my hunt."

"I do, actually." Amara was a close friend of Kyra's mother and an excellent tracker, so it made sense that she would have been asked to join in the Proving. It put Kyra's mind more at ease in trusting her new acquaintances.

"Feel free to say no, but would you join us when we leave for our hunt tomorrow?"

"I'd be honored to hunt with the Sisters. Though, I guess I'm surprised an outsider would be asked to go along on a Proving?"

"Understandable. As with mine, and most of our other Provings, we like to have someone who is not a Sister of Fianna with us. We look at hunts as cooperative experiences, whether alone or with a group.

For even if hunting alone, you must cooperate with the nature of your surroundings. Your senses. Your skills. We Sisters of Fianna focus on the communal aspects of the hunt. Hunting with others, an 'outsider,' as you put it. And while it may sound silly, you being from Ultarria, the place of my Proving, I see as a sign of luck. As if the Fates have brought us together." Seraphina took a sip of ale. "Also, since I don't know when I will be able to visit Ultarria again, hunting with someone from there is the next best thing. So maybe it's a little selfish on my part."

Kyra thought for a moment. She was on unfamiliar, dangerous territory. She had never hunted in swamps before. Even with her experience with vicious animals, there was always great risk, especially with ones she hadn't faced before. Hunting with a group might be wise, but she didn't know these individuals. Then again, Kyra had never heard anything bad about the Sisters. Amara certainly would have brought it up if her experience with them had been negative. It had been a long time since Kyra had hunted with a group, but there was something that seemed right about joining them. She weighed the options, and settled on which choice she thought was best.

"What time do we leave?" Kyra felt at peace with her decision.

"At sunrise. I'm glad you will be joining us." Seraphina smiled and lowered her head.

They ordered another round of ale.

"Kyra." Eliana spoke up.

Kyra realized that Eliana and Brielle had been mostly silent during her conversation with Seraphina. The two wards had whispered a few things to each other, but had not interrupted the conversation. Now that the business of arranging the hunt had been concluded, Eliana and Brielle could speak freely.

"Brielle and I were wondering why you seemed so interested in other farmer's story," Eliana said. "We overheard you talking to the magistrate."

"Pabiyan?" Kyra clarified.

"Yes." Eliana nodded. "The one that thinks it's a monster, or whatever."

"Well," Kyra began. "There's usually some kernel of truth even in the strangest of legends and stories. So, if there is something out there other than a krogall, we might get a little insight on what we could be hunting."

"That does make sense," Brielle responded.

The group shared hunting stories into the late hours of the night. The time came for sleep. The Sisters had already paid for a room. Kyra, not wanting to impose, got a room for herself.

Once in her room, Kyra set her things down and laid down on the bed. She took a deep breath, closed her eyes, and cleared her mind. She embraced sleep. Dawn would arrive soon.

***

Sunlight broke through the darkness as Kyra, Seraphina, Brielle, and Eliana walked to Pabiyan's farm. They had risen, had their morning meal, and set off before the sun had begun its rise.

They made sure to have the proper equipment for their hunt, especially the right arrows. Krogall skin and scales, while not impenetrable, were tough. Heavier, broadhead arrows would be essential. Draw weight would increase, slowing their rate of fire, but the wrong arrows would just bounce off.

They traveled fairly light. The swamps were dense with kyrus trees, making it impossible to take the hunting cart with them. The only thing that the Sisters carried with them, that Kyra didn't, were spears.

As they approached the farm, they saw a man tending a herd of gryats. The bleating from the herd carried through the otherwise quiet morning.

Kyra always thought gryats were silly looking creatures. Their single, centered eye. Their four small, multicolored horns that curled back. Their little beards. They looked like something a small child would draw if they were creating an animal. It belied their usefulness as their fur and hide made for well insulated clothing, and their milk and meat for sustenance.

The man tending the herd was tall and wiry. It was clear he had spent almost every day of his life outside. He turned towards the group as they approached.

"Pleasant dawn to you," Kyra hailed the man, as the other three also raised their hands in greeting.

"Pleasant dawn." The man spoke with some apprehension.

"Are you Pabiyan?"

"I am."

"I'm Kyra. This is Seraphina, Brielle, and Eliana. We wanted to ask you about what's been taking and killing your gryats."

Pabiyan stiffened defensively.

"Why? So you can make funna me?"

"No! Not at all!" Kyra tried to put him at ease. "We are hunting whatever it is that's doing this. It would be foolish of us to not avail ourselves of all the information available."

Pabiyan looked over the group. His jaw clenched and moved from side to side as he weighed the sincerity of Kyra's words.

"Alright." Pabiyan relaxed his shoulders. He shook his head, scrunched his lips a few times, appearing to chew the words before speaking. "So, I'm sure y'all know about the torn up gyrats and missin' people, so I'll spare ya that. And I know everyone thinks it's a krogall. But," he sighed. "That ain't what I saw. One night, maybe a few dawns ago, I heard rustlin' and my herd making a fuss. I had been stayin' up late tryin'a get eyes on or stop whatever was killin' my gryats. As I'm comin' out my dwellin' here, I hear singin'. Not like actual words, but like, sing songy hummin' or something like that. Sounds like a woman making that sound. I then hear the shriek of one a my gryat. I run to it, which, looking back mighta been stupid on my part, and I seen the zhu-trask slitherin' away back to the swamp. I know what a krogall is, and I know what a krogall aint. And that weren't no krograll." Pabiyan crossed his arms and shrugged.

Brielle spoke up first.

"Everyone seems so sure it's a krogall. Why do you seem so sure it isn't?"

Pabyian nodded and waved his hand, indicating the large pen area he was standing in.

"I'm sure you've noticed how everythin' is raised up, includin' this pen." Brielle nodded. "There's a few reasons for that. One is, when it rains here, it rains constant and for a long time. Makes the ground too soft, and floodin' too easy. Gryats can be stupid creatures, and have been known to get themselves stuck in the mud drown, 'cause they're too dumb to move to higher ground. This," he gestured around to the large elevated pen, "keeps them elevated. Natural grazing vegetation grows up through the slats, and everybody's happy. Another reason is it's much more difficult for a krogall to climb up and in. Now, it's not impossible for a krogall to climb up somethin', but these are designed to keep that from happenin'. Put that together with what I saw... No krogall I ever seen moved like that. Krogall do kinda slither and use their stubby legs to push along, but they're one long thing. What I seen? Top half was like a person from behind. Arms, and back, and head, and all that. Plus I seen the moonlight reflecting off its skin. Like it was water or something. Krogall skin don't ever look wet like that. They're scaly things. Not smooth or slick."

"So we are looking for a half woman, half... slimy thing?" asked Eliana.

"I mean, basically, yeah," Pabiyan responded. "Look. I understand I might be wrong, and it ain't a zhu-trask. But it sure did fit the old stories. And whatever is out there is dangerous. Other hunters ain't come back out them swamps." He sniffed the air and looked towards clouds only he could see. "The rains are gonna start soon too. When that happens, it's easy to lose track of time and direction in the swamps, 'cause you ain't gonna see the sun for a while. So, you know, be extra careful."

"Thank you, Pabiyan." Seraphina smiled sincerely. "We will try and put an end to these troubles, one way or another."

"I certainly hope you do." Pabiyan appeared grateful, which, Kyra assumed, came from their willingness to listen to him without judgement. "Good huntin'."

The group took their leave and headed to the swamps.

There wasn't much of a trail to follow. The rains prior to their arrival on Braethous assured that, so they followed the direction Pabiyan had indicated.

The kypr trees became more clustered as they entered the swamp proper. Brielle removed a ribbon from her satchel and tied it to a tree. She affixed it with the knot facing the direction from which they had come. Eliana checked to make sure the knot was secure. She nodded, and the group continued on.

The group stayed in relative silence, keeping eyes and ears open for any sign. There would be the occasional hiss and rustle of a standard krogall as it would sprawl and drag itself away. Sporadic caws and cries from flying swamp creatures peppered the air. The fluttering of wings as those feathered animals flew away broke up the monotony of the buzzing and chirping of insects.

Every fifty paces or so, Brielle would tie a new ribbon, Eliana would check it, and they would move on. Any change in direction was a straight line. Careful not to zig zag in their approach, the group kept formation. Each moved within a few paces from the other, spread out enough to cover a decent amount of territory, but never too far that another wouldn't be able to get to them quickly.

The sun had made it about halfway in its journey across the Braethian sky when the rains came. The deep blue and streaks of green were hidden behind slate colored clouds. While no deluge, it certainly made things more difficult for the hunters. And, if Pabiyan was correct, it would be like this for the next several sunrises. The Sisters pulled up the hoods of their jerkins and Kyra donned her own hooded cloak.

They pressed on.

The swamp became more gloomy as the day went on. Still beautiful in its way, but melancholy in spirit.

They continued deeper into the swamp, being sure to mark their trail and check for any signs of a large creature. They didn't expect to find anything the first day. Usually, something that big would be deep within its habitat, needing denser surroundings for coverage.

Their pace was slow. The unfamiliar territory, coupled with their extra caution, limited their movements. They stopped briefly for rest and a light, midday meal before continuing on until darkness overtook the sky.

The group found the driest and most elevated spot they could to set up camp. Seraphina and Brielle arranged torch stands while Kyra and Eliana worked on getting the fire going. After trimming away the outer wet layer of the wood, they angled the wood over the kindling and methodically adjusted until the fire burned stronger than the light rain could affect.

They ate in relative silence. Learning the sounds of the environment and being aware of any changes was too important to allow for chatter. They limited their discussion to arranging watch shifts. Seraphina would take first watch, followed by Kyra, Brielle, and Eliana.

Seraphina started her patrol while the others settled in as best they could to sleep. Kyra felt the fatigue from the day start to overtake her. Thankfully, it superseded the discomfort of the sleeping conditions, and she was soon asleep.

Darkness surrounded her. Not the darkness of a forgotten dream, but some tangible void where a dream should be.

Kyra was unsettled. This was wrong. Her hunting experience soon made her aware of something else in the void. Something lurking deep within the dark. Something deadly, and desperate to devour. From somewhere far within the abyss came a snort and a growl, as if from some giant beast.

Kyra woke with a start. Her eyes darted about. She needed to reorient herself. The fire. The torches. Brielle and Eliana sleeping. Seraphina keeping watch. Kyra exhaled slowly and calmed herself. She nodded in response to Seraphina's whispered question if she was alright. Reassured by her surroundings, Kyra relaxed, though didn't sleep, until it was her watch shift.

Thankfully, Kyra's watch passed without incident. Sounds of the swamp kept her company and helped keep her mind focused on things other than her dream. That presence had been filled with such a desire to destroy. Filled with so much hate. She pushed it from her mind. Her attention needed to be on her immediate surroundings. Kyra patrolled until it was time to wake Brielle to take over.

Kyra laid back down as Brielle began her shift. The remaining hours of sleep for Kyra were, mercifully, without dreams.

***

Kyra woke up at dawn. At least, as far as she could tell, it was dawn.

The sun was still hidden behind the cover of clouds and rain, which had not stopped since it had started the day before. There was barely enough light to turn the darkness of night into the gloomy grey of day.

Kyra stretched and shivered, causing droplets of rainwater to scatter off her cloak. She felt mildly stiff and cold. She rubbed the rest of her sleep away from her eyes with the back of her hand.

Eliana had already begun to prepare the morning meal, since she had the last watch. The others rose and helped her finish.

After the brief morning meal, the group doused the fire, made sure they had all their equipment, and continued deeper into the swamp.

Kyra's thoughts occasionally slipped back to her dream. She usually wasn't one to obsess on such things, but there was something sinister there beyond a normal nightmare. However, there were more immediate things to focus on. Kyra was thankful for the hunt to keep her distracted from her other nagging thoughts.

The start of the day proceeded just as the previous. Carefully traversing the swamp. Marking their trail. Looking for any sign of an abnormally large krogall, or another creature. They stopped briefly about mid day to eat and rest, then continued on their way.

As they moved deeper into the swamp, the kypr trees were much larger. The knees of the kypr trees protruding from the ground were more frequent and increased in size as well. The muddy ground of the swamp became more arduous and there was a growing amount of standing water.

Eliana suddenly raised her hand, stopping the group. She gestured everyone forward and pointed to something at the base of a tree.

The other three gathered around.

"Is that...?" Bewilderment coated Brielle's whisper.

Kyra, who had crouched down to look closely, nodded.

"It's shed scales and moulted feathers." Kyra was amazed and impressed by what she saw.

"Those are enormous." Brielle shook her head.

The dead scales stuck against and between the knees and tree were at least twice the size of any they had seen on the krogalls so far.

Eliana had hunched down as well to inspect the scales.

"Even this dead layer is thick and tough." She tapped the scales. "The krogall that shed this must be an armored monster."

"The good thing is something that big won't be easy to miss on land."

Seraphina had been keeping a look out. "But the standing water has been getting deeper. It's possible we are heading towards a large body of water, if so..."

"We could end up right on top of it if it's hiding out in deep water." Eliana finished the statement.

"Exactly," Seraphina confirmed.

Kyra looked at the others. They shared a nod confirming they were ready to move on. Eliana took point again, joined by Kyra, while Seraphina and Brielle brought up the rear.

"How long have you been a hunter?" Eliana asked, keeping her eyes scanning the ground and her voice low.

> ***" I held a hand against my stomach. A lurching feeling turned my organs, like that first drop on a roller coaster after having just gotten used to the upward climb.***

"Practically since I could walk," Kyra answered. "My parents were both hunters, so I guess it was a good thing I took to it. And enjoyed it. You?"

"I started when I was around twelve cycles. My family are mostly artists, which I still love to do, but something about this life called to me."

"Were they supportive?" Eliana nodded.

"Thankfully. Maybe a little disappointed, but they weren't going to stand in the way of my pursuit."

"How did you join the Sisters?"

"There are other hunters outside of the Sisters of Fianna, but they are the elite. Kind of the highest honor on Paralia to be accepted into the Sisterhood. They train all comers though. Very much want to make sure you not only have the skills, but the love for the hunt as well. We are also always encouraged to develop our other interests, like art, farming, music, cooking, whatever. You know. Be a well rounded person, or something like that." She laughed lightly. "Plus, I think it helps you if you wind up not being initiated as a Sister, or realizing that the hunt isn't for you. Gives you something to go to instead of, I don't know, emptiness of failure."

"Makes a lot of sense. I guess I just assumed the Sisters of Fianna were more militaristic, I guess?"

"Oh, no. Nothing like that. Don't get me wrong, it's not easy. And their standards are high. Not everyone makes it to the Proving. And not everyone passes either. We all have our strengths and weaknesses, so a lot of it is showing how you will strengthen the Sisters of Fianna with your particular skills. Like, I'm probably a better tracker than Brielle, but she's definitely the better shot. And the better cook. She should probably be taking the last watch, now that I think about it. Better morning meal."

"You're probably right," Kyra joked. Eliana stuck out her lower lip in a feigned pout.

"Look." Eliana pointed then to crushed and bent typha. "Seems our beast slithered that way."

Kyra helped Eliana tie a trail marker before the group set off in the new direction.

"But, yeah," Eliana continued the conversation, "if for some reason I failed my Proving, I have something to go back to. I'd be sad and disappointed, obviously, but not devastated. You know? The hunt is a huge part of our lives, but it isn't the only thing." Kyra nodded.

"Seems to be a balanced view of it."

"What would you do if you weren't a huntress?"

Kyra thought for a moment.

"Honestly? I don't know. I supposed if pressed I'd say farming? With some dabbling in herbalism as well."

"Really?" Eliana asked with interest. Kyra nodded.

"I learned a little bit from the wise women and healers in Undera, the village near where I grew up, so maybe that?"

"It's an incredibly useful skill to have." Eliana squinted and nodded her head as if she were strengthening the argument for her agreement in Kyra's theoretical pursuit. "I suppose you could continue that study and not give up the hunt."

"I suppose you're right." Kyra smiled.

"What of your parents?"

"They, uh. I..."

“Shh.” Eliana raised her hand then pointed. Kyra exhaled a long, deep breath through her lips, thankful to have been cut off.

Seraphina and Brielle joined them as they came to a large body of water and what Eliana had pointed to. A herd of wild gyrat.

The water. The food source. Perfect place for a large creature.

Kyra’s musings were interrupted, and confirmed, when the monstrous krogall burst through the surface of the water. It clamped its jaws down on a gyrat with such speed and force, the smaller animal had no chance of getting away.

The giant krogall was as frightening as it was impressive. A regular krograll could kill a person fairly easily. This beast would have no problem. Like its smaller counterparts, the monster’s scales were iridescent, showing off swampy greens, blues, yellows, and reds. The feathers growing on the legs were of similar colors, rivaling the beauty of many airbourne creatures. This was a killer though, and they couldn’t afford to make any mistakes.

Since the krogall could move any which way once it became aware of the four’s presence, Seraphina and Brielle moved through the kypr trees, arching their way left to get to the other side of the krograll.

Eliana set her spears to her left, poised to be grabbed, then readied her bow.

Kyra nocked an arrow and moved a few steps to her right.

Before they could fully get in position, one of the bleating, fleeing gyrat circled and ran in their direction. It tripped, getting stuck on something in the mud, and began bleating louder.

Eliana shot the gyrat with an arrow to silence it, but it was too late.

The giant krogall, still hungry and looking for an easy kill, had already begun its acceleration towards the gyrat. The beast moved with unbelievable quickness. It was upon Kyra and Eliana almost before they could react.

Kyra let loose her arrow, embedding it into the shoulder of the krogall.

Unphased, the giant continued it’s slithering sprint towards them.

Kyra nocked another arrow and lept back, launching herself off of kypr knees. She loosed her arrow into the krogall. There was no way of outrunning the animal. They were going to have to kill it now, and quickly.

Seraphina and Brielle, having watched the krogall charge Kyra and Eliana, released their arrows into the hindquarters of the creature. The krogall stumbled, but soon resumed its hurtle towards Kyra, jaws wide open.

Eliana saw the beast almost upon Kyra. She grabbed her spear and dashed towards the krogall.

Kyra released another arrow at the krogall and dove out of the way at the last second.

As the krogall slowed to snap its jaws at Kyra, giving Eliana enough of an opening to drive her spear into the base of the krogall's neck.

The beast flipped and started thrashing. Eliana's spear snapped. She was propelled backwards from the force of the krogall's writhing. She fell to a seated position before rising weakly to her feet. She took several steps backwards, and fell. Mud and water splashed around her, soaking her.

The krogall went still as Seraphina and Brielle approached, arrows at the ready.

Kyra crept forward as well. She stood, another arrow nocked, next to where Eliana sat in the mud.

Seraphina looked at Kyra and Brielle to make sure they were ready. They nodded in response. Seraphina kicked the tip of the kograll's tail.

Nothing.

They all relaxed. Brielle moved quickly to bind the kograll's jaws shut with rope, just in case. Kyra, after putting her arrow back in her quiver, extended her hand to Eliana, who clasped it. Kyra helped pull her off the ground to her feet.

"Nice work." Kyra said in all sincerity. She was impressed with the decisive action Eliana had taken.

"Thanks!" Eliana partially smiled, her pride obscured beneath a bit of bashfulness.

"Are you both alright?" Seraphina was concerned. Kyra and Eliana nodded.

"I should probably help Brielle." Eliana excused herself and began aiding Brielle in preparing the krogall for transport out of the swamp.

“What are your thoughts on their hunt?” Seraphina asked Kyra.

“They’re good,” Kyra answered honestly. “Seem to know their stuff on tracking. And reacted the best they could have given the situation.”

Seraphina nodded. “I agree. Obviously I would have liked a better setup, but they handled an imperfect scenario fairly well I think.” She smiled proudly.

Brielle and Eliana, after retrieving what arrows they could, tied a rope harness around the krogall’s upper body and front legs. The ends of the rope extended and were tied around a makeshift yoke made from Eliana’s remaining spear and one of Brielle’s. Ropes were then tied to the krogall’s hind legs as well.

The krogall was heavy. While it helped that the krogall was a creature built to slide through the mud and water, dragging it out of the swamp would still be a chore. Eliana and Brielle took the yoke on their shoulders. Kyra and Seraphina shouldered a rope each, and the group began retracing their steps out of the swamp.

They had made it only a few paces when a strange mist began to creep in around them. It billowed in from all sides. It was thin and wispy about their feet, but rose and grew thicker, soon enveloping them in a fog.

The fog, dense and cold, continued to build. It moved eerily, like it had some kind of conscious intent. It soon swallowed the group completely. Kyra could barely see two paces in front of her. The rope slipped out of her hands, and off her shoulder. She stopped and called out to her companions.

Nothing.

She felt disoriented. Had she changed directions? How much time had passed? How could they have gotten so far away that they couldn’t hear her?

Kyra was conflicted. She told herself she should stay put. The fog would eventually clear, and then she could figure out which way to go. But she also felt compelled to move; to find a way out of the fog. She thought she heard a voice calling her name in the distance.

“Eliana? Seraphina? Brielle?” Kyra called out.

Her feet began to take her in the direction of the voice. She moved as if in a haze, not fully under her own control. Her boots plodded heavily as she trudged along.

Kyra wasn't sure how far she had gone when she had begun to hear singing. There were no discernable words. It was more of a sing-songy type humming.

Kyra pushed the haze from her mind. She stood in an open area within the swamp. Water just covered the tops of her boots. The fog cleared, save for some steam rising off the large, shallow pool of water she stood in. Kyra saw the source of the singing.

It had its back to Kyra. The creature's lower half was long and scaled, though flat, smooth, wet, and slimy, unlike the krogalls. It had no legs. Its lower body was all tail. From the waist up, it was much like a person. Though the same wet and slimy hue covered its mottled skin, the same colors as the muddy swamp.

It was the zhu-trask to be sure.

One of its arms was outstretched, its hand on the head of an emaciated man.

The man was stuck to a tree by some dried, mucus-like bindings. He was shriveled and drained, like a husk. Another man, in a similar state, was to the left of the zhu-trask.

The zhu-trask lifted its hand off the man, and turned towards Kyra. The grotesque half woman-half creature smiled.

"Ahh. Another morsel finds its way into my home." The zhu-trask slithered slowly towards Kyra, sloshing the water as it moved. "I prefer the sustenance of fear, but your sorrow will do just as well." She darted towards Kyra with such force and speed, that Kyra barely had time to react.

Kyra dove to her left, but was struck across the chest by the lashing tail of the zhu-trask. She splashed down into the water, winded from the powerful blow. She immediately tried to scramble away. She was facing the zhu-trask in its lair, making the challenge of fighting a clearly intelligent creature even more difficult.

Before Kyra could fully get her footing and move to a more advantageous position, the zhu-trask was upon her. Its cold, moist hands wrapped around Kyra's neck. The creature lifted her up and snaked its way towards the trees where the two men were trapped.

Kyra kept one hand on the disgusting flesh of the creature's arm, trying to keep herself lifted enough to minimize the strain on her neck. Her other hand reached for her knife. Kyra managed to unsheath the blade and, with all her strength, buried it into the arm of the zhu-trask.

The zhu-trask shrieked, and dropped Kyra.

Kyra fell with a splash. Briskly, she righted herself and attempted to sprint out of the water to more stable ground.

The zhu-trask was upon her again. It struck Kyra with the back of its fist, knocking her down again. Kyra pushed herself back, dragging herself backwards through the water. The zhu-trask approached, methodically this time, toying with its prey.

"Kyra!"

Seraphina's shout was enough to snap the zhu-trask's attention away from Kyra, who used the split second to get up again and run.

A hiss escaped from the mouth of the zhu-trask. It pursued Kyra again.

An arrow flew into the side of the zhu-trask. The creature turned towards the source of the pain. As it pulled the arrow from its gelatinous flesh, one of Seraphina's remaining two spears found its way into the creature's chest. The zhu-trask screamed, snapped off the shaft of the spear, and yanked the spearhead from its body.

Seraphina had already begun to charge the zhu-trask, her last spear in hand. The water splashed beneath her feet as she rushed the vile creature. Seraphina dropped to her knee, avoiding a swipe from the zhu-trask arm, and impaled the creature on her spear. The spear punctured through the stomach and out the back of the zhu-trask as Seraphina released her grip on the spear and skidded past the shrieking creature.

Brielle followed from the opposite side. She charged and then leapt into the air, plunging her own spear down through the back of the zhu-trask. The spearhead lodged into the muck below, pinning the zhu-trask in place.

Kyra had been able to steady herself during Seraphina and Brielle's spear attacks and had strung her bow. She, along with the other three women, nocked an arrow.

The four raised their bows. In unspoken unison, they loosed their arrows into the head of the creature.

The zhu-trask twitched in its death throes, then fell limp.

Kyra exhaled in relief and bent over at the knees. She rested her left forearm against her thigh and her right hand above her knee. Her left hand still gripped her bow. She felt a hand on her shoulder.

"Are you alright?" Seraphina was concerned. Kyra nodded.

"I'm glad you all showed up when you did."

"Thankfully, you left easy footprints to follow."

"Is it dead?" Kyra nodded towards the zhu-trask.

"Let's hope so."

Kyra stood up straight again. She and Seraphina walked over to where Brielle and Eliana were investigating bonds of the captured men.

Though unwell and drained, the men were still alive. The more coherent of the two whispered desperately.

"Help us."

The four women carefully chipped away at the dried mucu and freed the two men. While the others helped the men carefully sit and regain some strength, Kyra searched for her knife. She used an arrow to poke around in the water and muck, hoping to tap the solid shape of her knife. After a bit of searching, her arrow made contact. Kyra lowered her finger tips straight down, careful to locate the hilt before gripping the knife to retrieve it. After lifting it from the water, she wiped the blade off out of habit and sheathed it before rejoining the other three.

"They should be able to travel soon," Brielle said of the men. "This one said they were hunters, so that mystery is solved. There are other bodies behind the trees, but..." She shook her head. She didn't need to finish for the others to know they had found the missing villagers.

"So what do we do with that?" Seraphina nodded towards the zhu-trask.

"We could cut its head off and take it back with us." The other three looked at Eliana, shocked at her statement. "What? Undeniable evidence."

The others thought for a moment, then shrugged in agreement.

Kyra and Seraphina set to the process of beheading the zhu-trask while Brielle and Eliana prepared the two hunters for travel. Kyra snapped off the shafts of the four arrows, leaving the arrowheads embedded in the skull of the creature. Her knife cut through the neck of the zhu-trask easier than she would have thought. Once finished, she and Seraphina wrapped it in blankets.

"The body?"

"Burn it."

They doused the body of the zhu-trask in the fluid used for their torches and set the body ablaze.

The huntresses led the two men back to where the Sisters had left the body of the giant krogall. They retrieved their prize, and began the slow journey back to the village.

The two hunters, after some rest and food, confirmed that they had gone after whatever had been plaguing the village and had gotten lost in a fog before they too stumbled into the lair of the zhu-trask. Though it would probably be quite a while before their full recovery, just being free from the zhu-trask had already brought strength back to the two men.

After following the trail markers they had left, the hunting party arrived back at the village.

Villagers, upon seeing the giant krogall and the returning group, sent a murmur of amazement cascading throughout the village. Word had already reached the magistrate by the time Kyra and Seraphina went to speak with him.

They left the two men to be looked after, and while Brielle and Eliana stored the krogall on the Sisters' skiff, Kyra and Seraphina entered the village hall.

"Ah!" Magistrate Bardon greeted them. "I hear you have returned with the corpse of a giant krograll. I assume this was the beast that was causing so much terror to our village?"

"Not exactly."

Kyra set their bundle down on a table and unveiled the zhu-trask's head within. The magistrate gasped and stepped back in shock.

"Is that...?" His words trailed off.

"Yes. Turns out your legends were real."

Bardon shook his head in disbelief.

"I... Well... It seems I owe you all a significant bounty and unending gratitude." He paused. "I owe Pabiyan a sincere apology as well it seems.

Well, anyway, give me a moment and I will return with your payment. Split four ways, I'm assuming?" Seraphina nodded. "I shall return then."

Kyra wrapped the head back up in the blankets.

"What will you do with that?" Seraphina asked.

"Burn it. Like we did the body. Not sure I want to keep it as a trophy. Unless you want it." Seraphina shook her head.

"Some things just need to be destroyed."

The magistrate returned.

"Here we go." He handed over four bags of coin. "Thank you again. Obviously, you are all welcome to stay as long as you like, but if not, safe journeys to you."

Kyra and Seraphina bowed their heads slightly, then took their leave. They walked to the Sisters' skiff, where Brielle and Eliana were just finishing up preparations for departure.

"Where do you think you will go next?" Seraphina inquired.

"I'm not sure." Kyra sighed. "Probably just see where the winds take me for now." Seraphina smiled understandingly.

"You will always be welcome on Paralia, should your journeys bring you our way."

"Thank you." Kyra smiled, happy to know she was accepted and had a place to go if need be.

"It was an honor to hunt with you, Kyra."

"The honor was mine."

They grasped forearms in farewell.

"Blessed hunt."

"Blessed hunt."

Kyra bid farewell to Brielle and Eliana in the same fashion, then watched as their skiff left the harbour and disappeared into the sky.

After watching her new friends depart, Kyra paid her fee to the harbourmaster, and lifted off from the port.

She maintained a course still within the atmosphere of Braethous, low and slow enough to open the back of the *Tressa IV* without worry. Kyra had placed the blanket wrapped head of the zhu-trask in a container, and prepared to cremate it. The words the zhu-trask had spoken bothered Kyra. It had sniffed out the sorrow that Kyra thought she kept well buried. This, as well as thoughts of her dream and coupled with the knowledge of the blight, made Kyra worry. She was not naive to the fact of evil throughout the known realm, but these hints felt different.

Kyra pushed the thoughts away and set fire to the blankets. The smoke billowed out the back of the skiff. Once satisfied that the head had burned away, she closed and sealed the container. Outside Braethous's atmosphere, she would jettison it out into the great vastness of space.

The task done, she removed her armor and hunting gear. It would all need a good cleaning to remove the muck and filth from it.

Once clean, and in fresh clothes, Kyra set the Tressa IV to just drift a while. She wasn't sure where to head next, though deep down she knew that soon she would need to return home.

***

SUGAR WATER

by Blake Slaughter

At times I feel a phantom; others a
phenomenon. Like a spirit
transformed and humanized by
western culture, I'm back from the
dead just to sit in my grave with the
eyes of millions encroaching.

The necessities are within me and
more. I am sweet to the taste and
deadly in abundance. If you dare to
find me, I can provide a light or
inferno with the wave of a hand. I
am the king of a broken promised
land. Fascists roam the streets
seeking to overthrow me. The
barriers I've built will not detain
them.

My offspring may bear no
resemblance, but they might
continue the warfare against
opposing forces. Through blood and
through vengeance I will prevail
until I die- and that, my naive friend,
is the difference between them and I.

RIVER KIND OF DAY

by Gabriel McLeod

There was a buzzard free as a broken string kite flying by,
No monkey on its back,
No hunger in its belly, no tricks in its eyes.
For today feels like a River kind of day with cool blue breezes
Where the sun doesn't warm but shines
Like a new day, like a hooky day
Like something waiting around the corner to make you smile kind of day.
I am held back by a corner and a time clock
But can see my car looking over her shoulder at me
In the parking lot like a chocolate pony ready to ride.
Because the highway doesn't care
And the train howls down nearby tracks like a drunken cowboy
And the sky does not cry and the River keeps rolling on by
Somewhere out there, ever moving, ever changing,
waiting for me to flow just the same.